D'ANNIFERA PUBLISHING

Adults Love Coloring Too

SUMMER DREAM

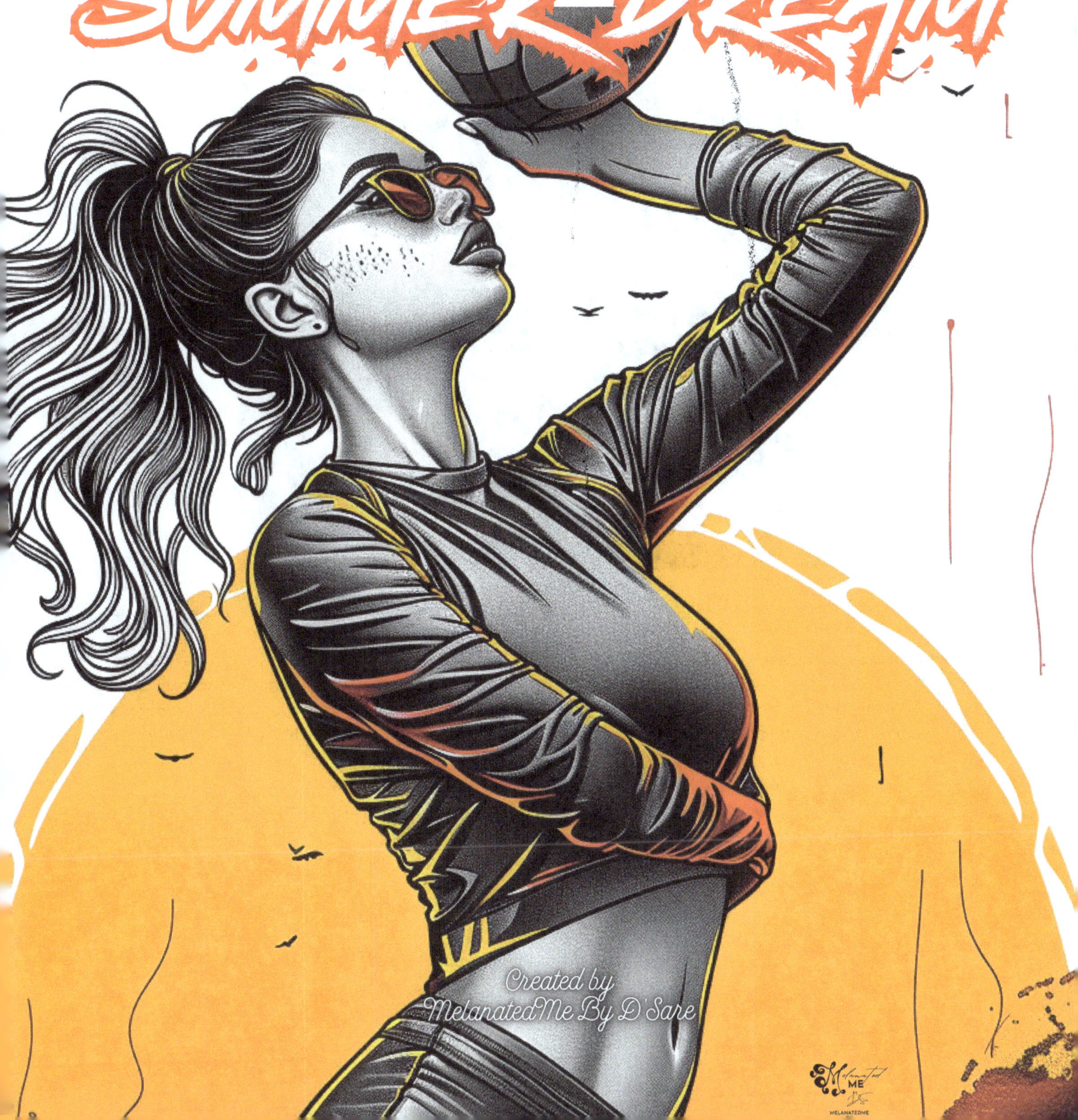

Created by
MelanatedMe By D'Sare

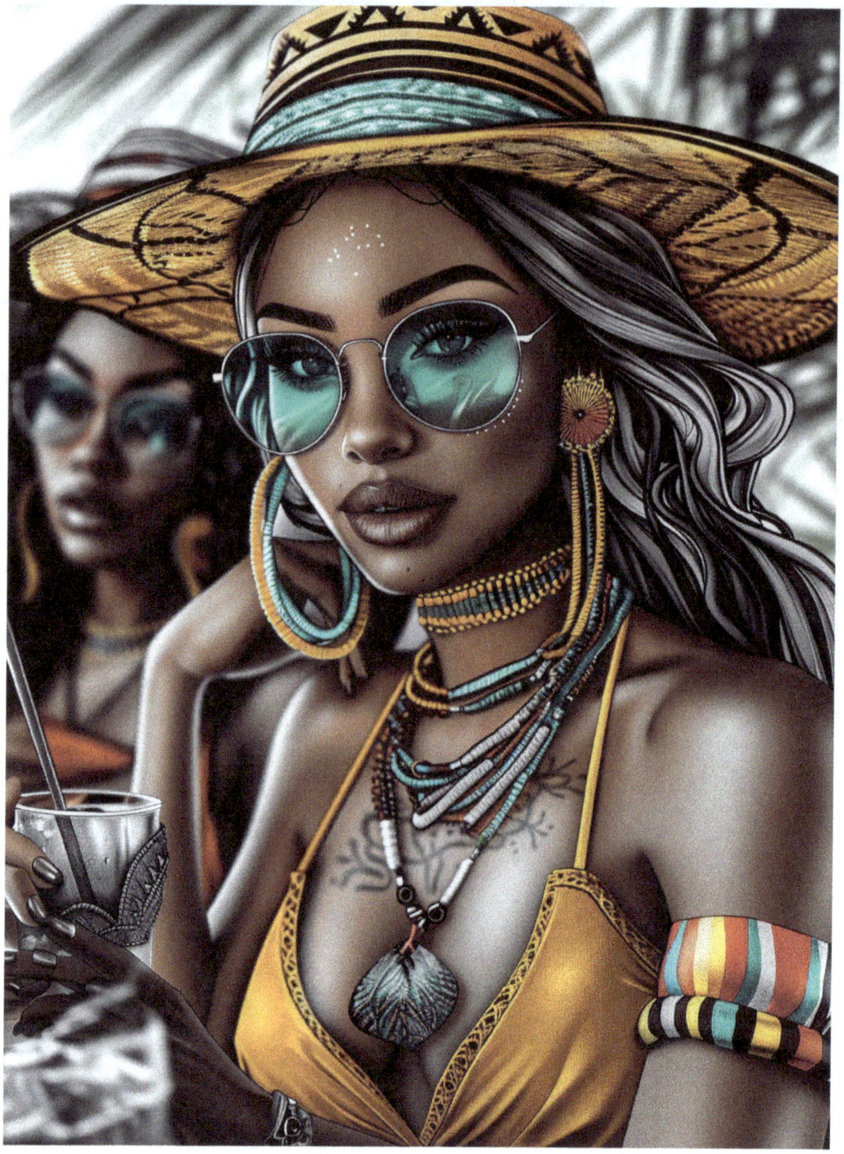

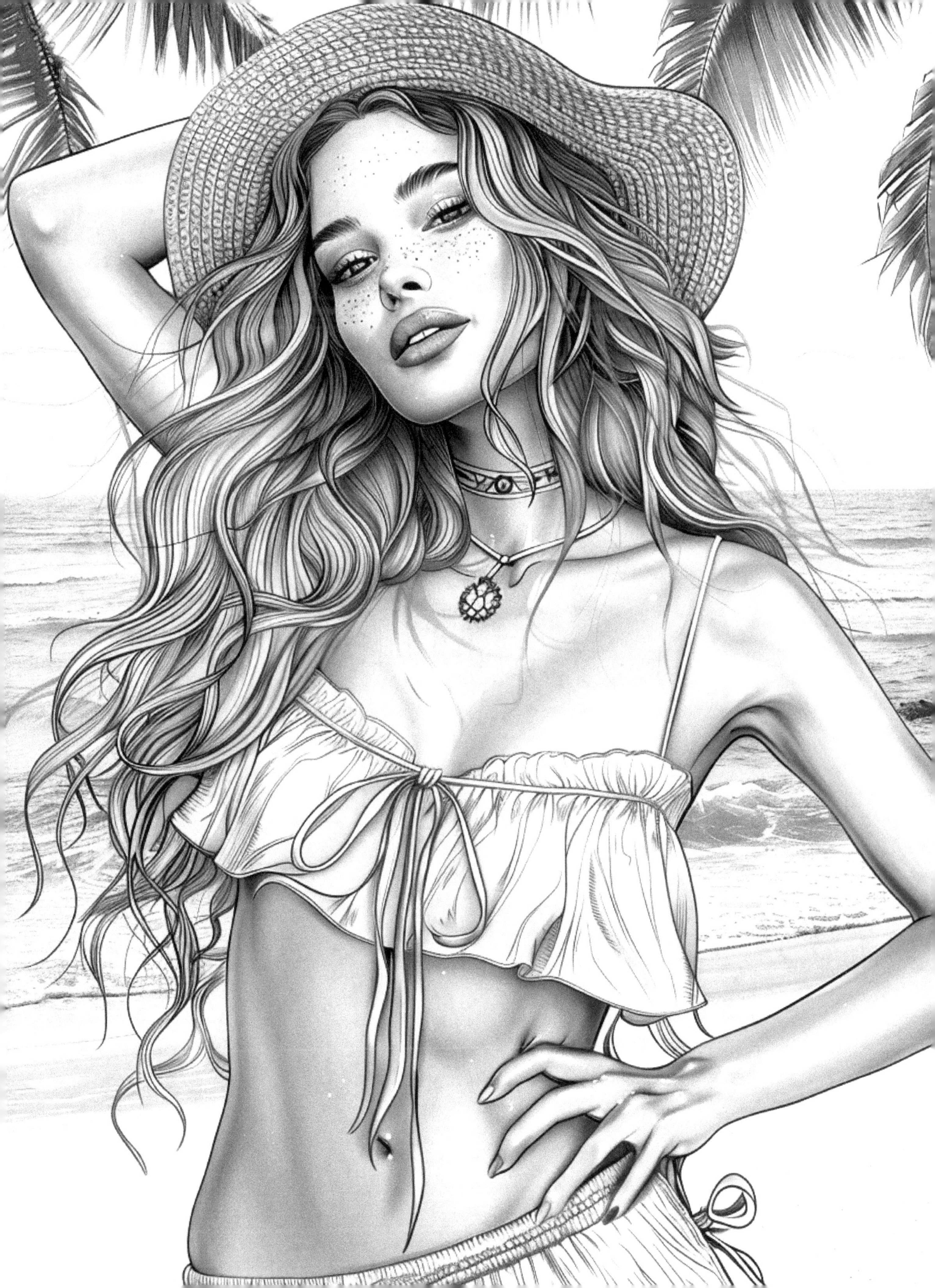

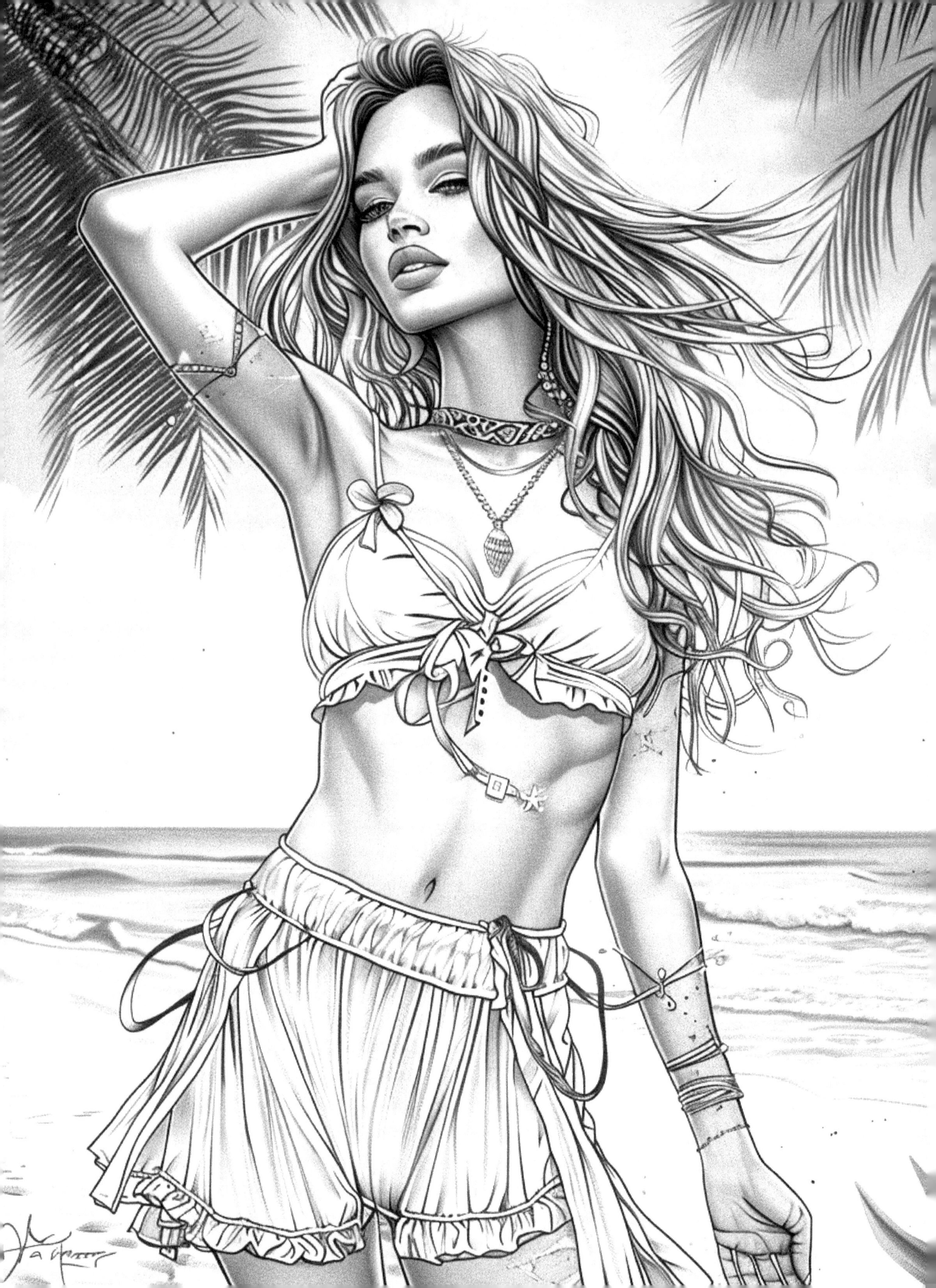

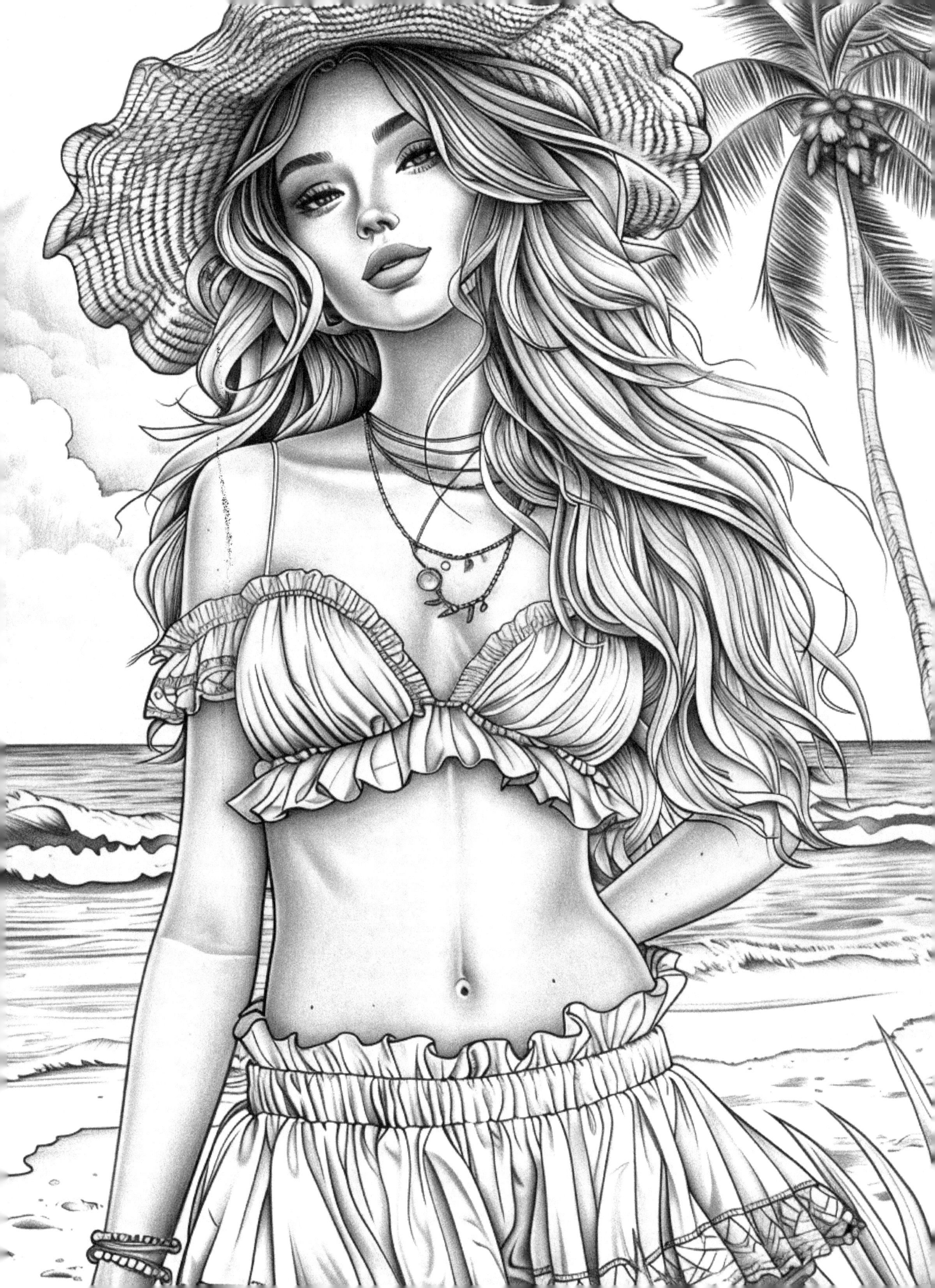

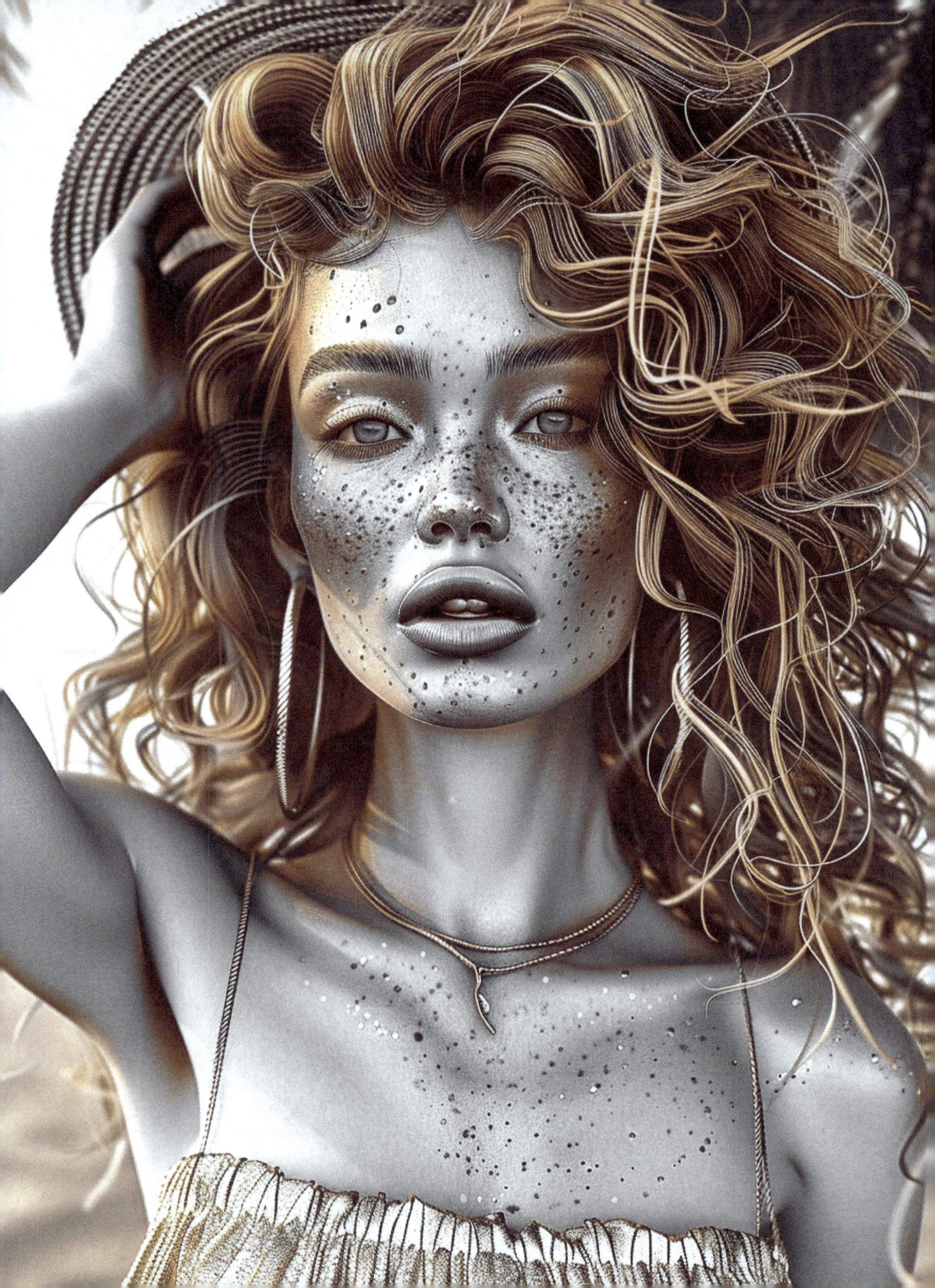

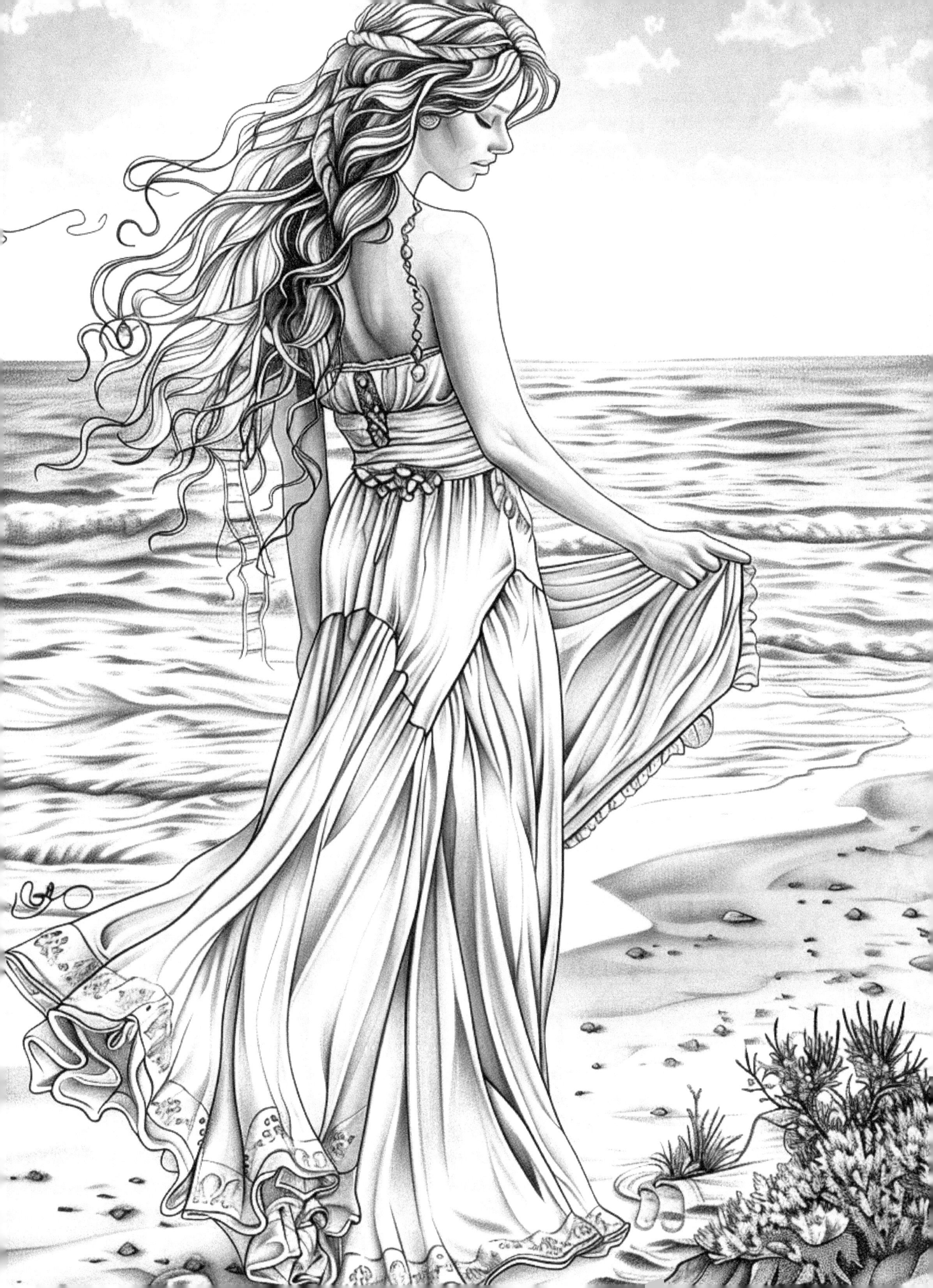

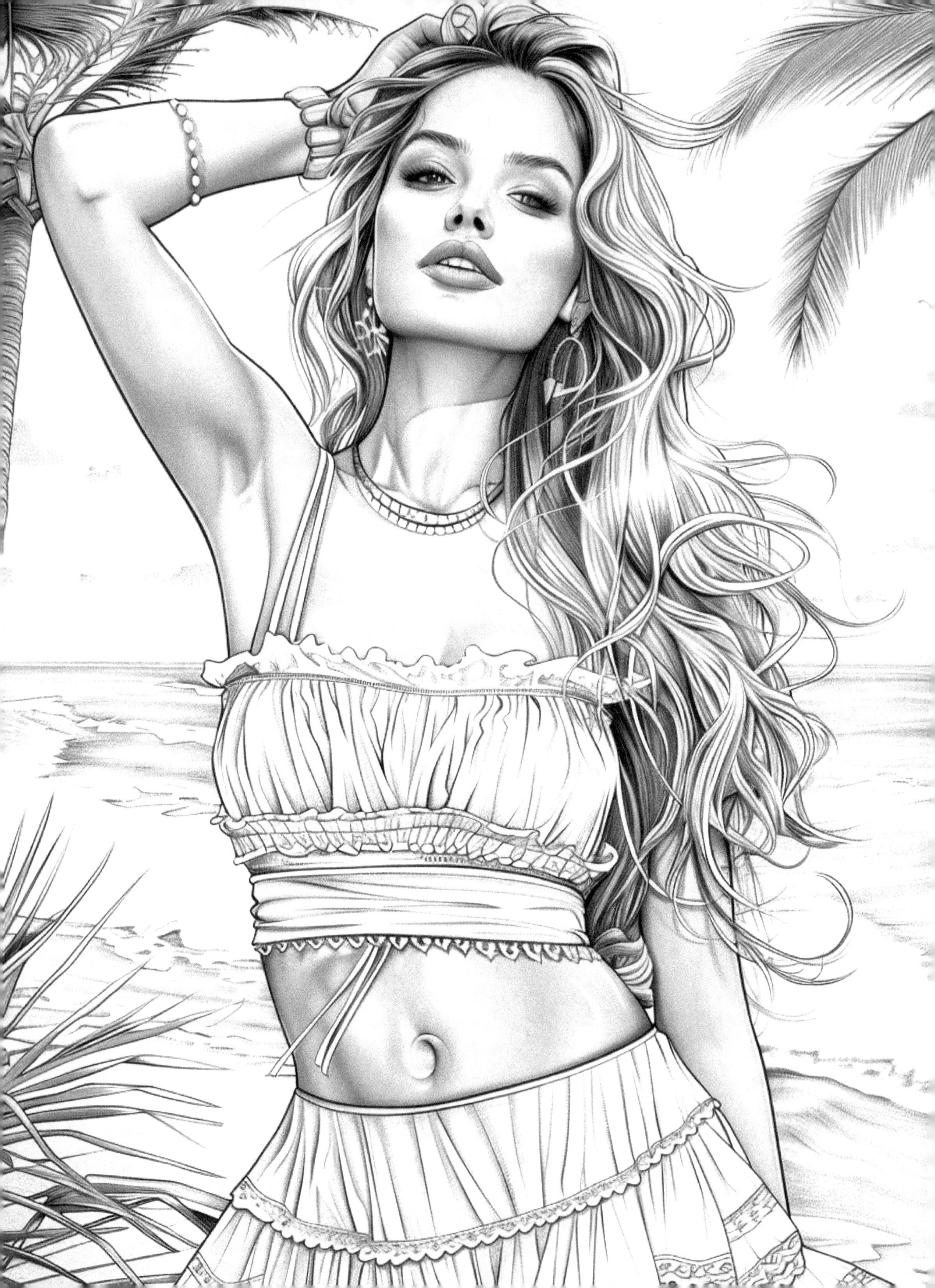

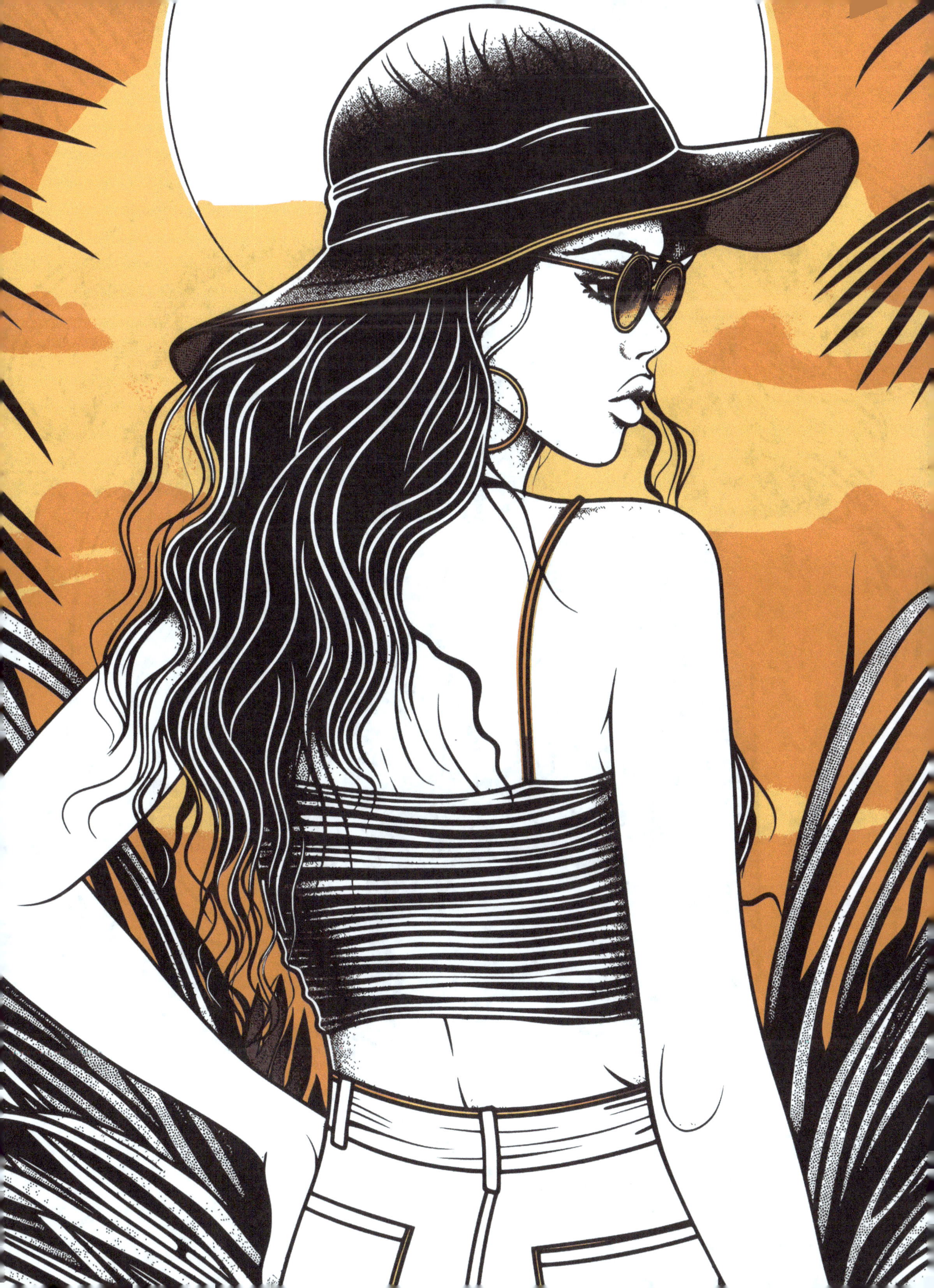

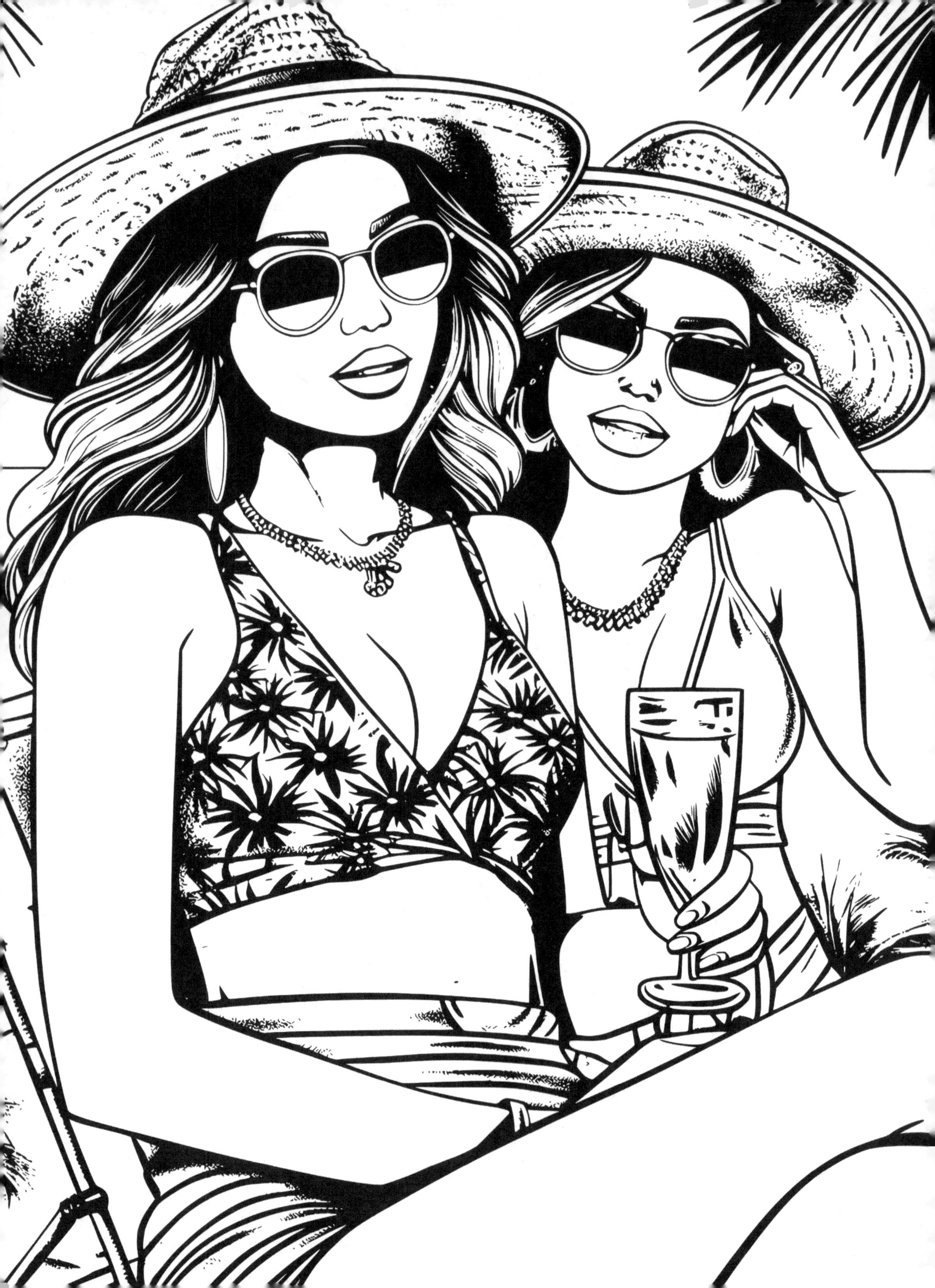

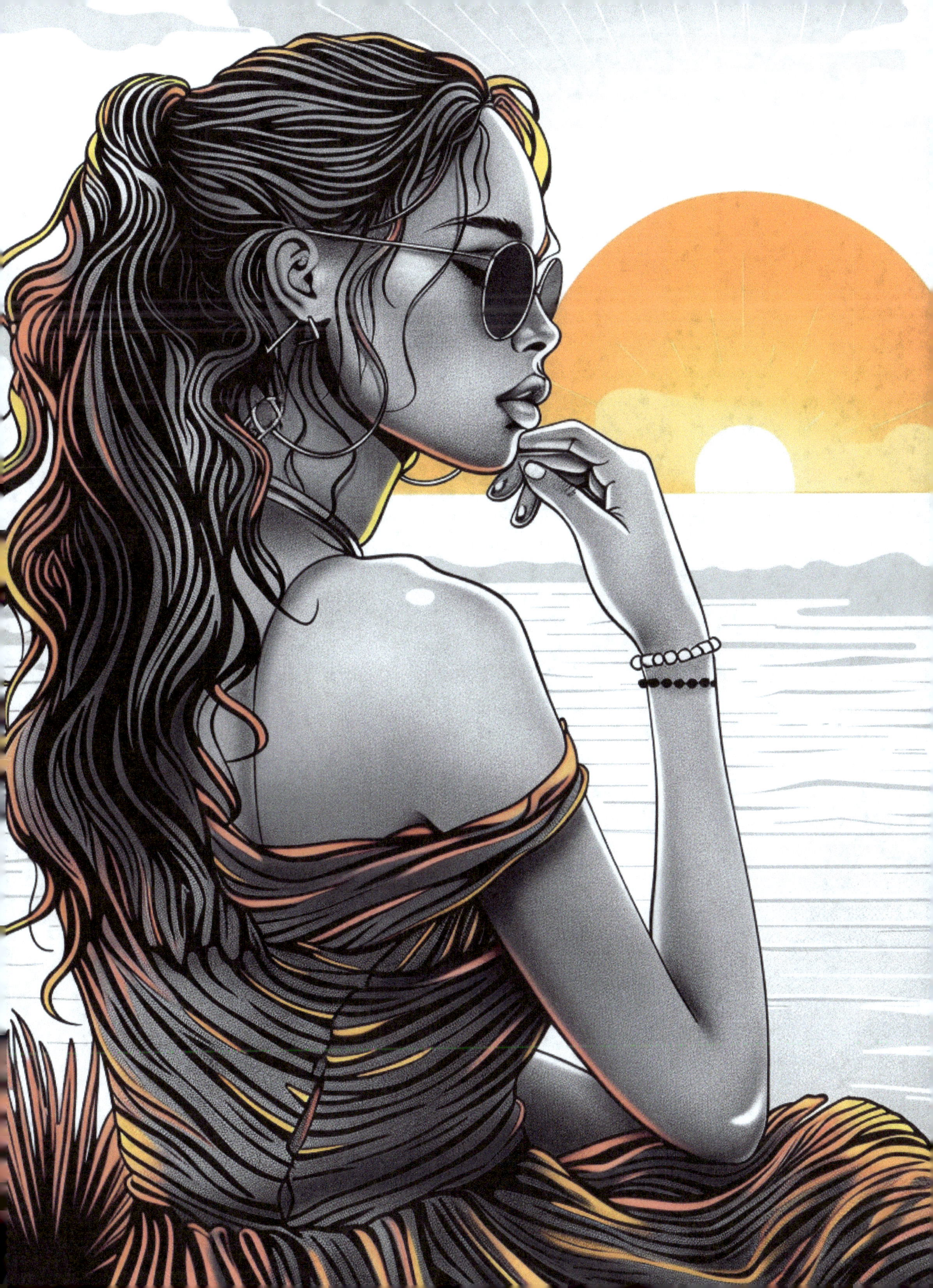

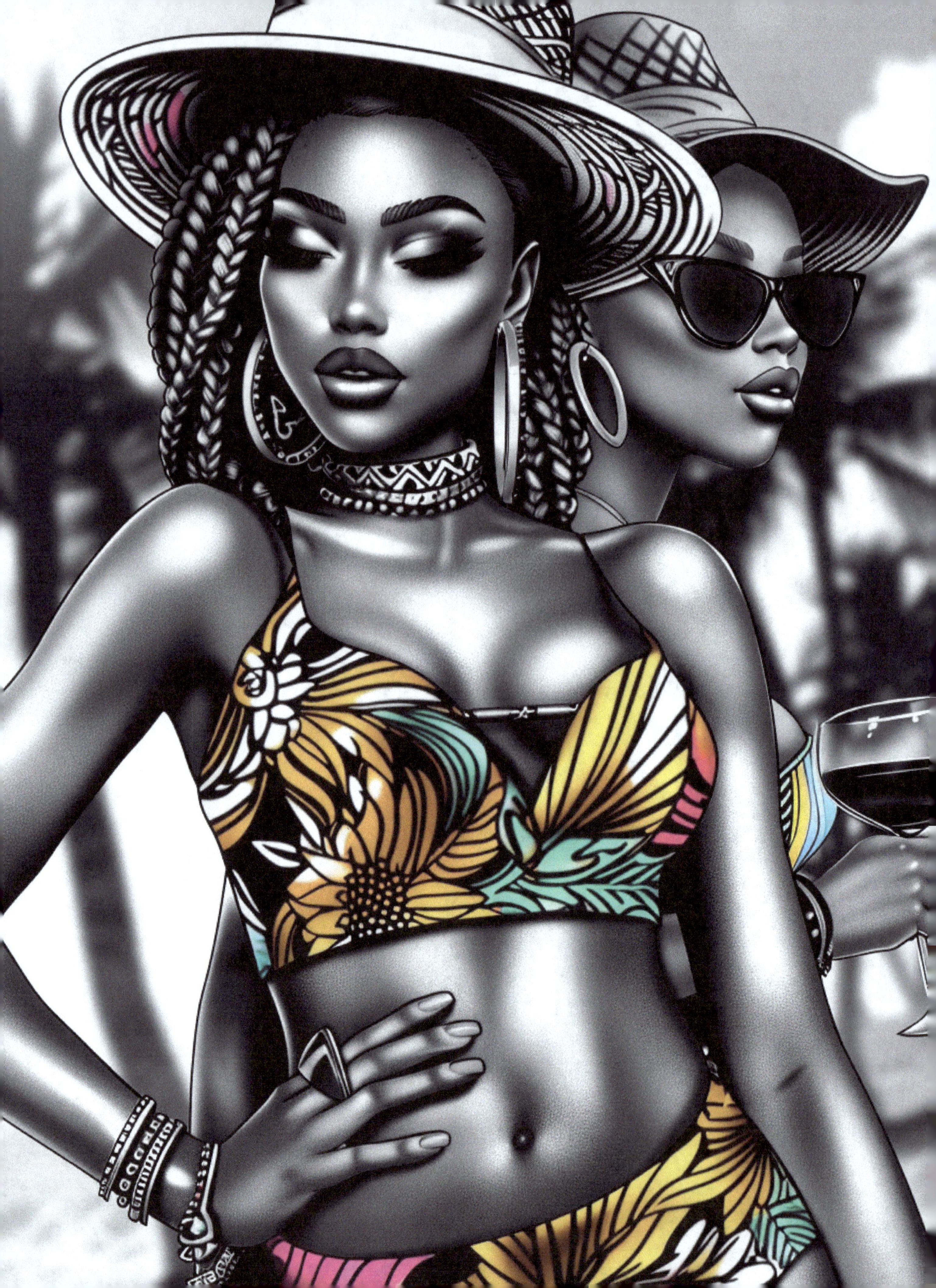

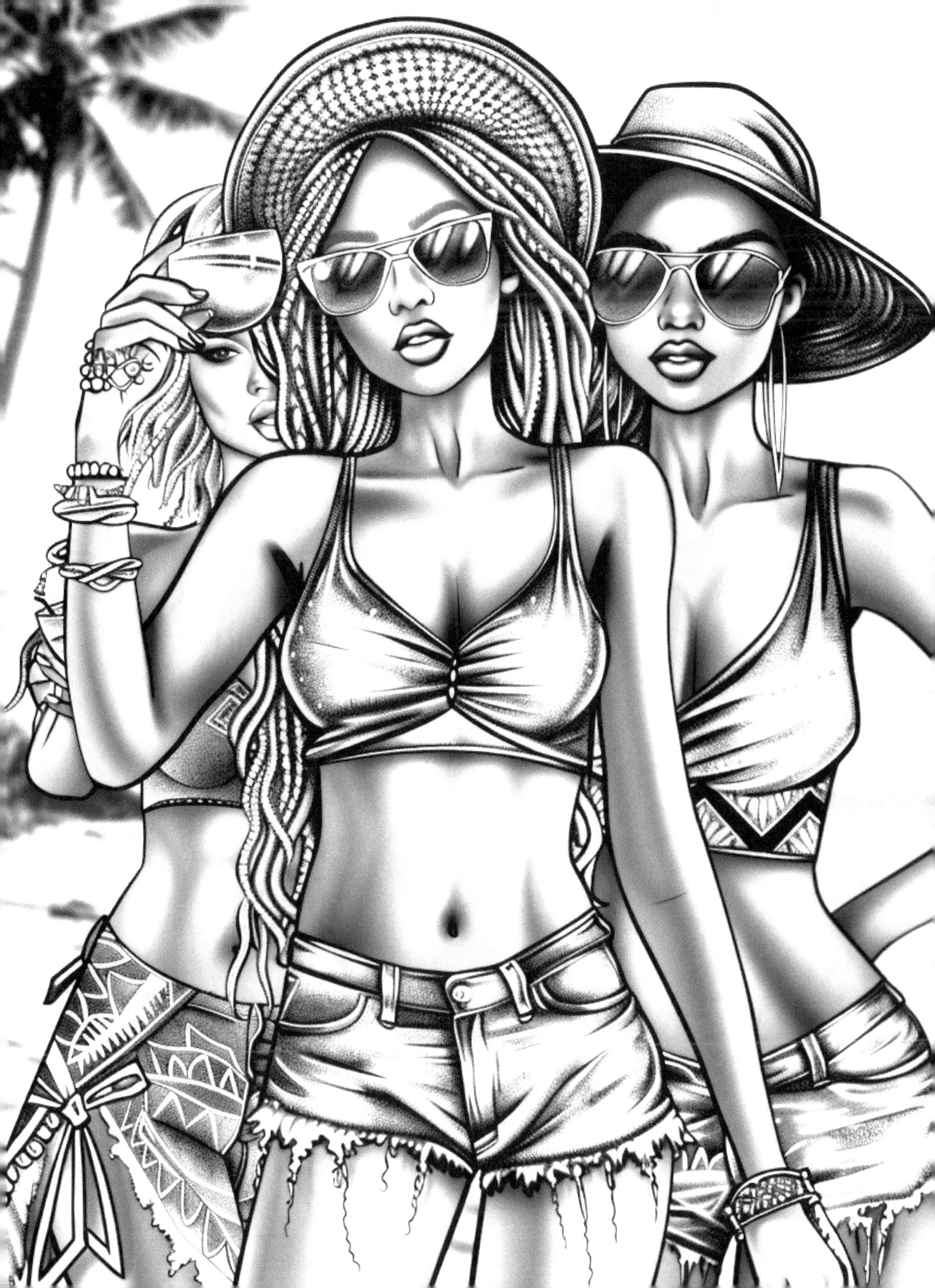

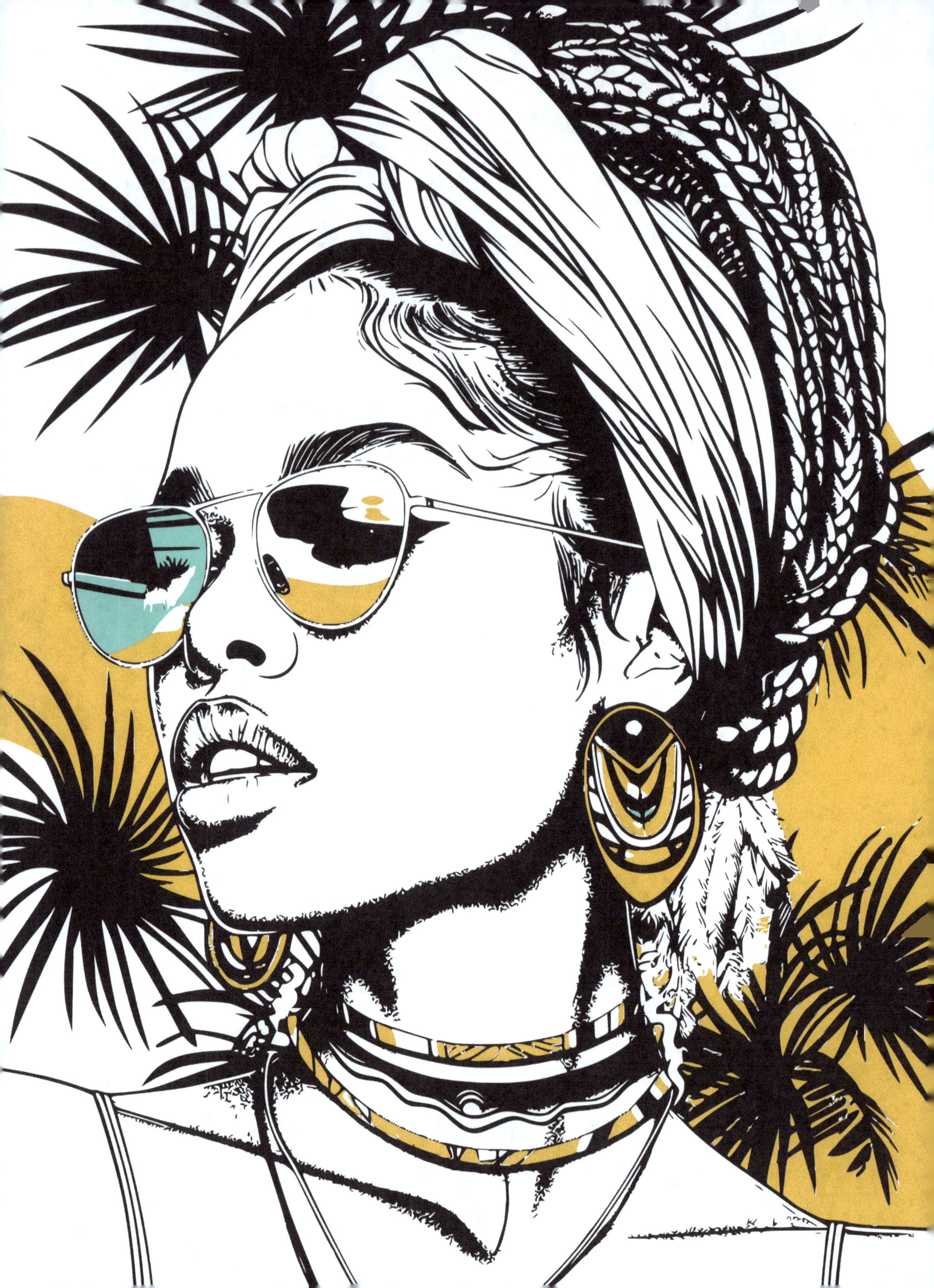

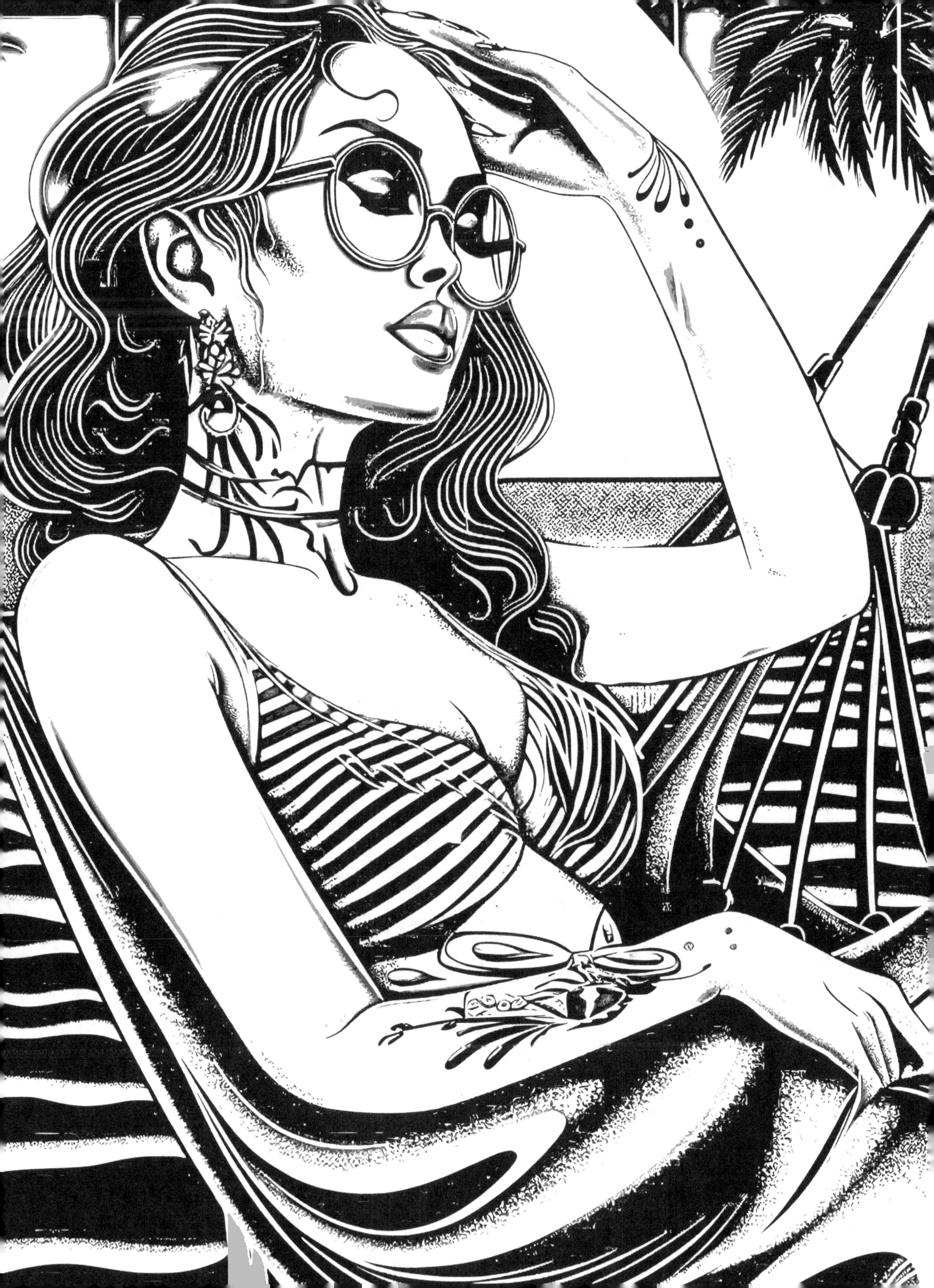

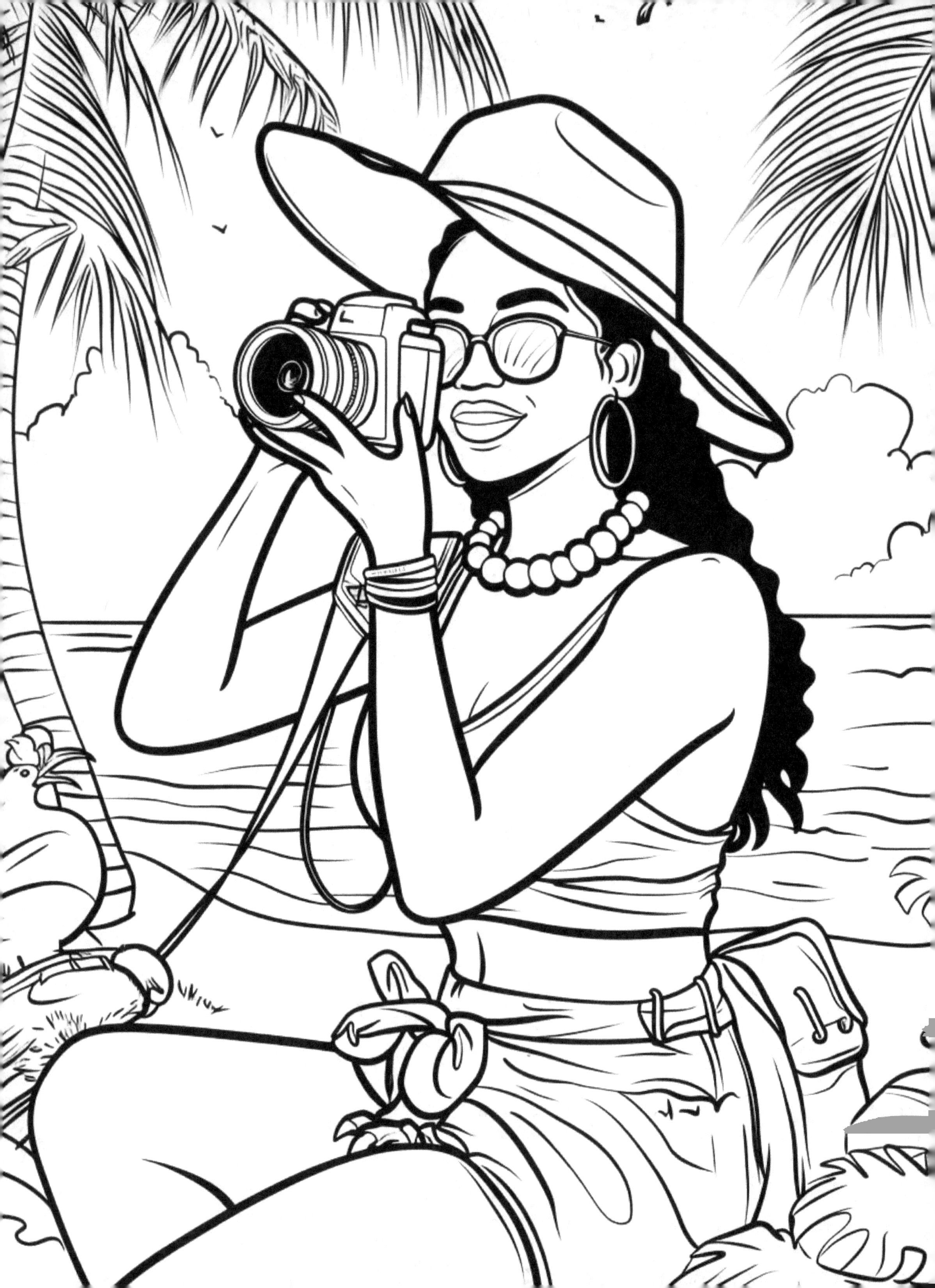

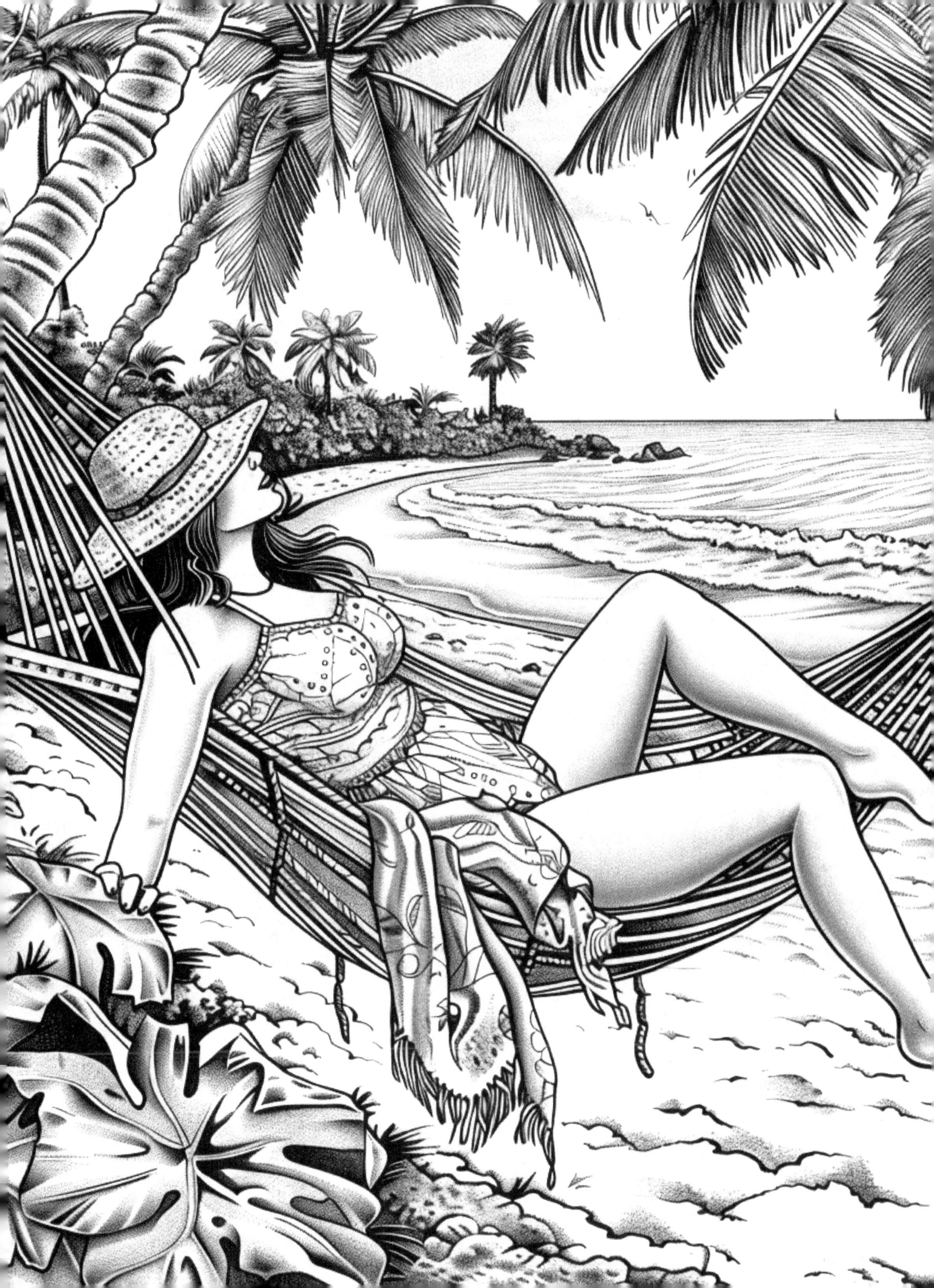

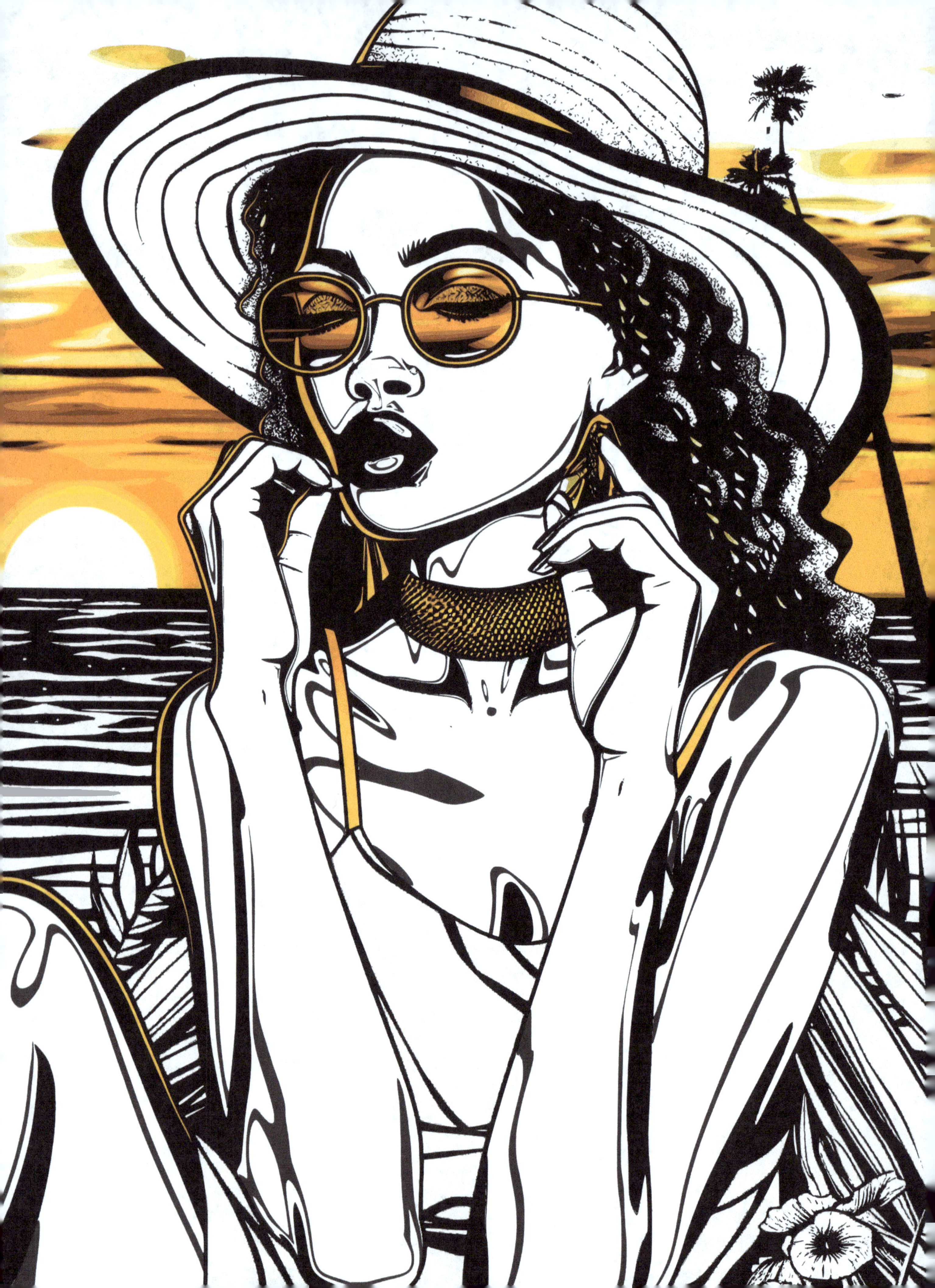

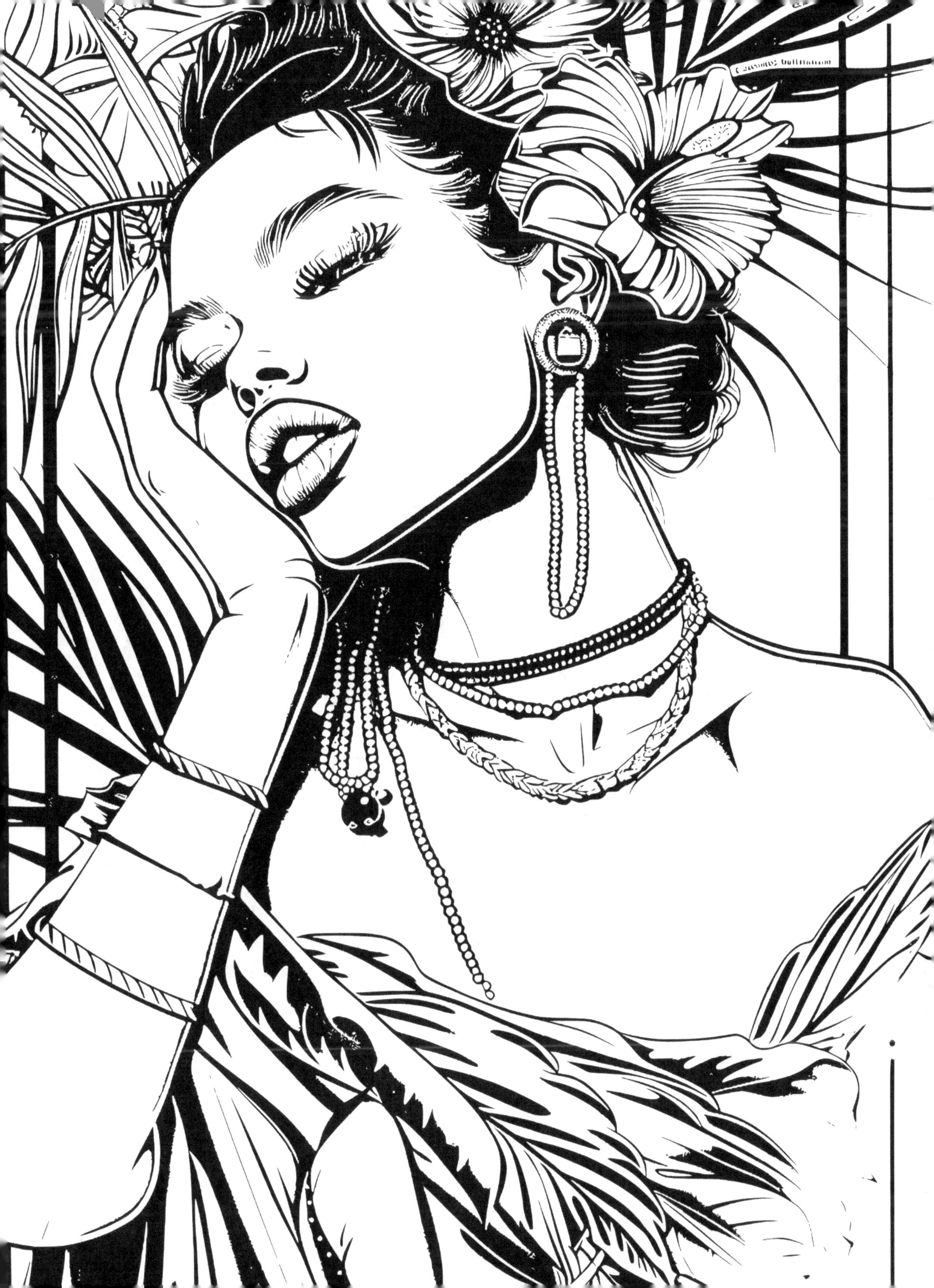

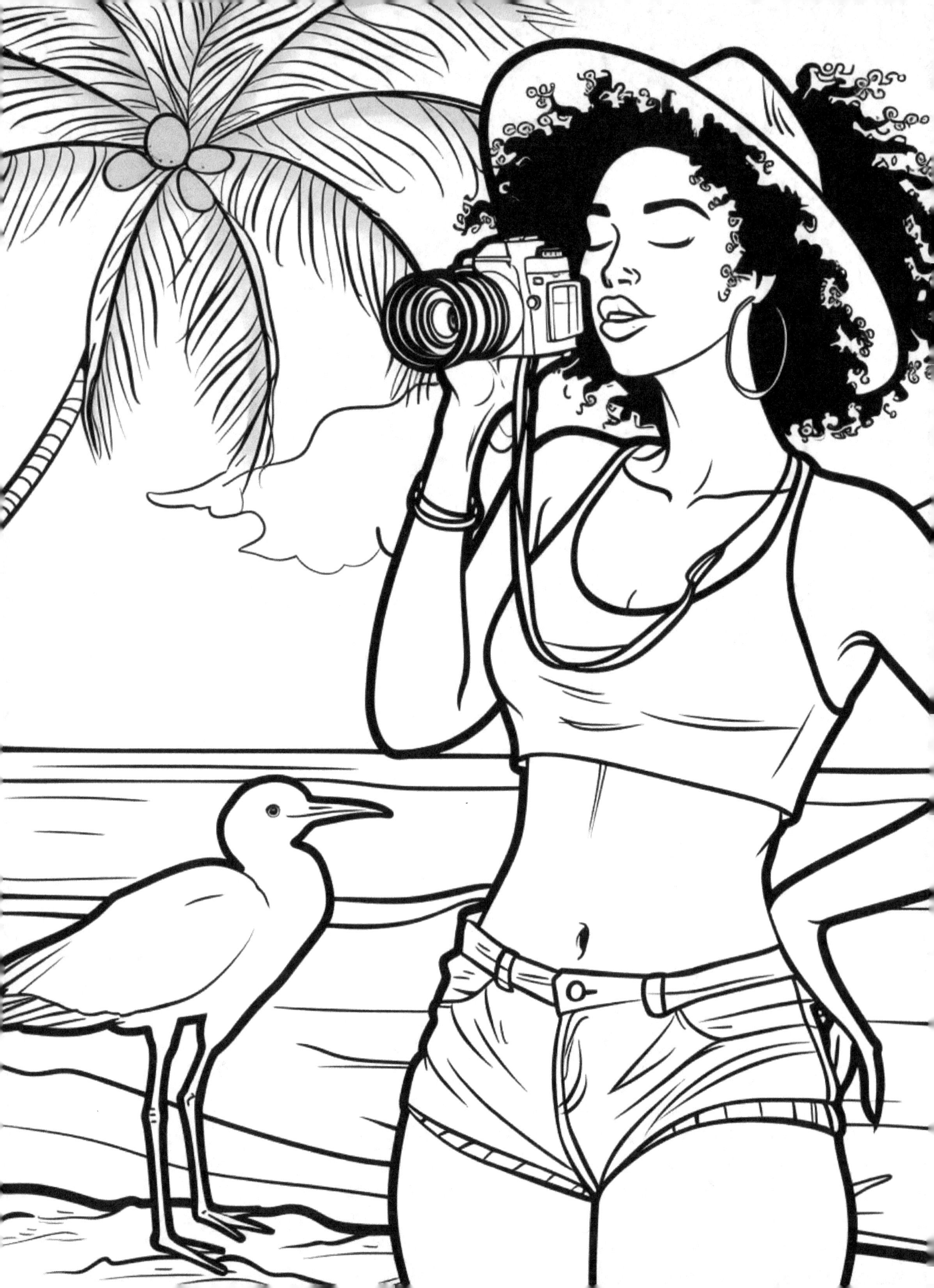

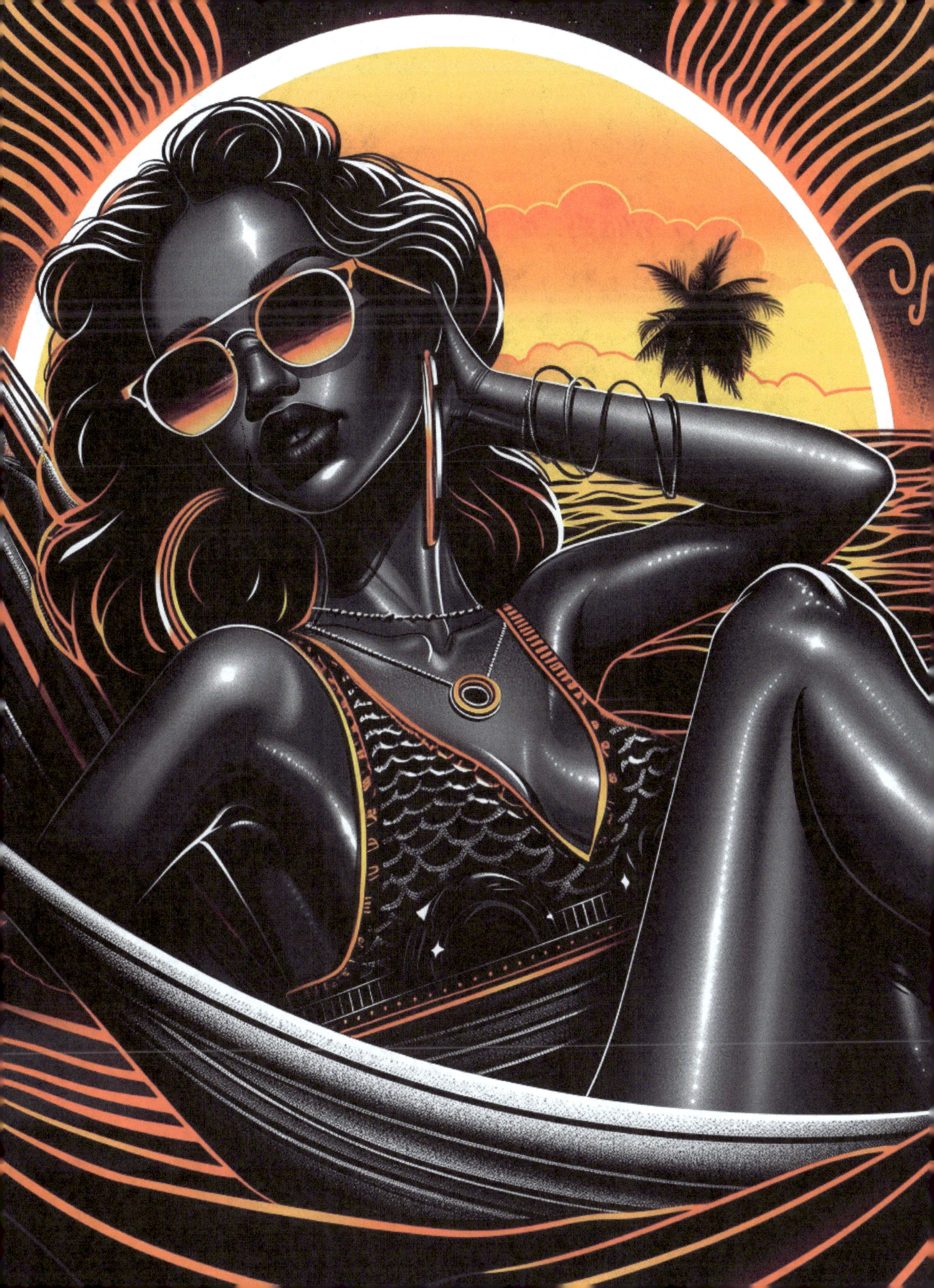

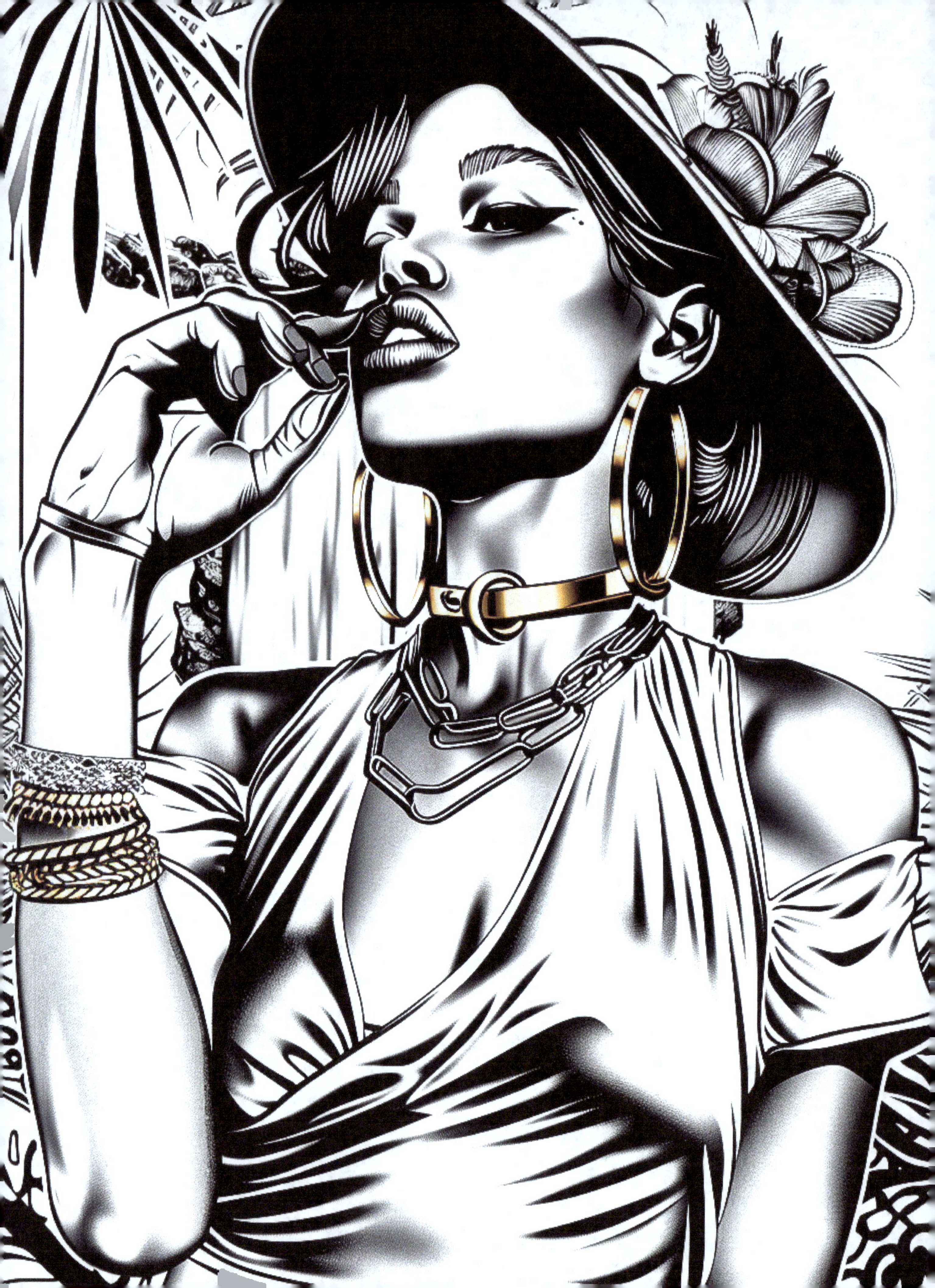

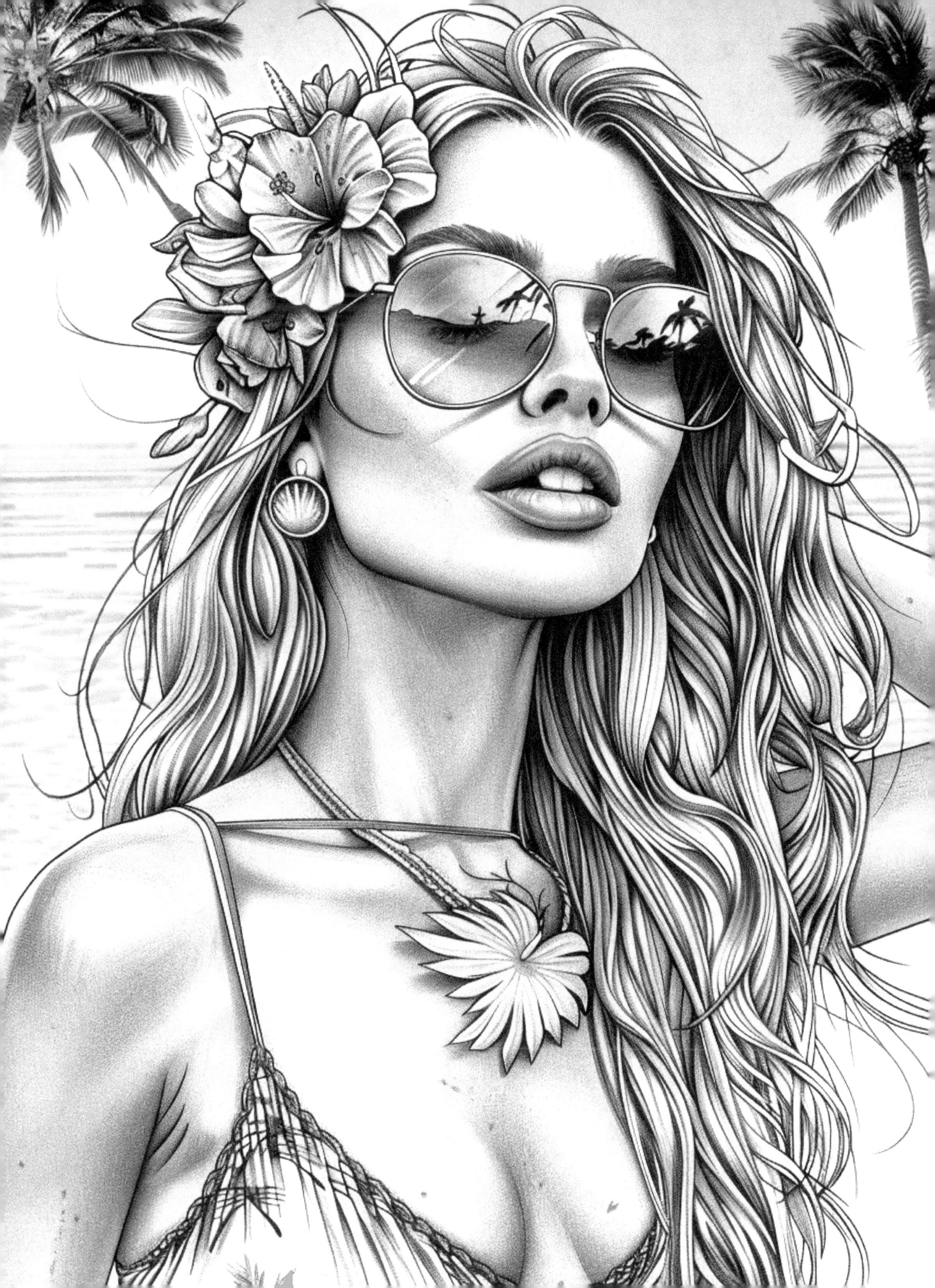

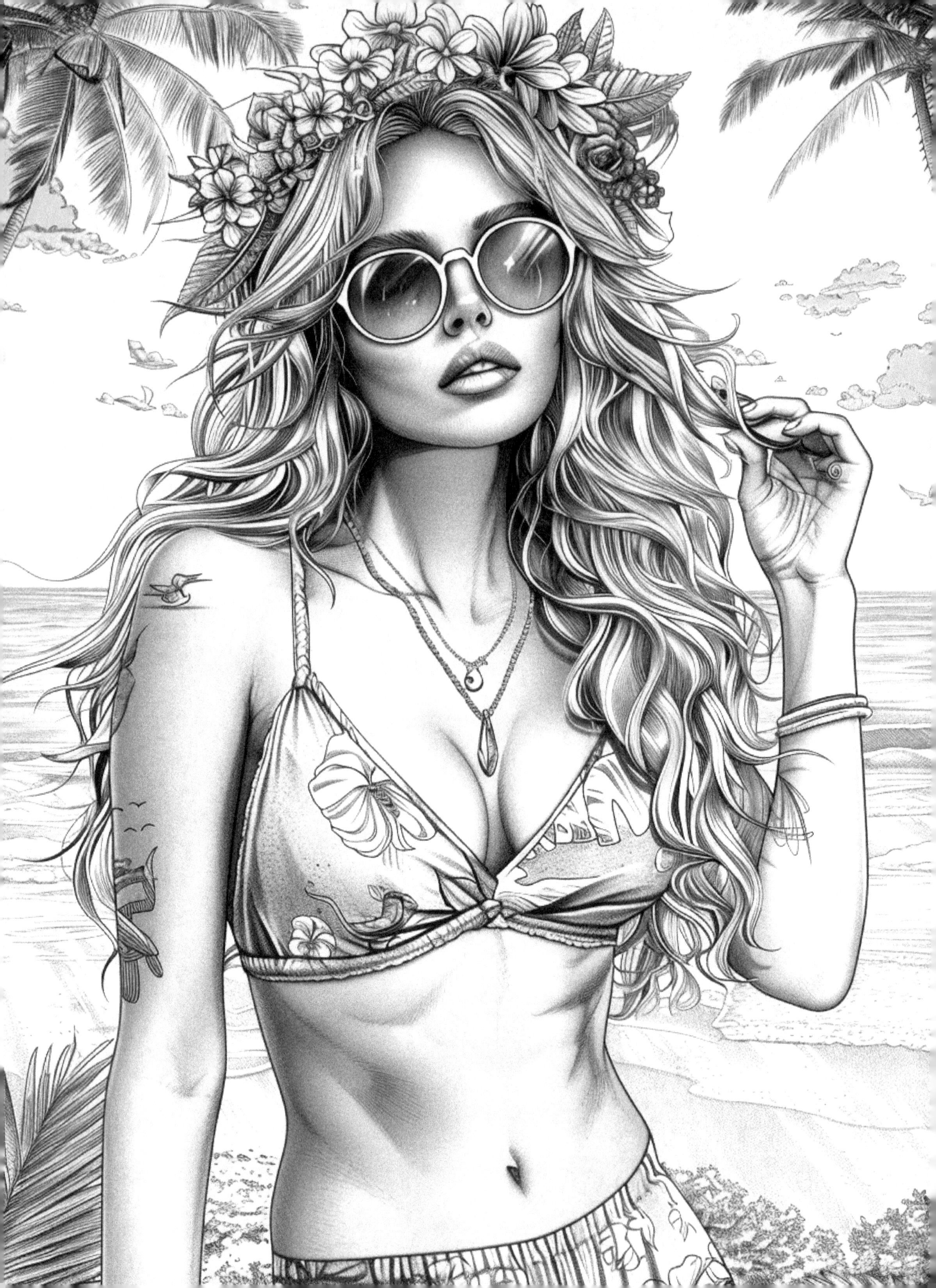

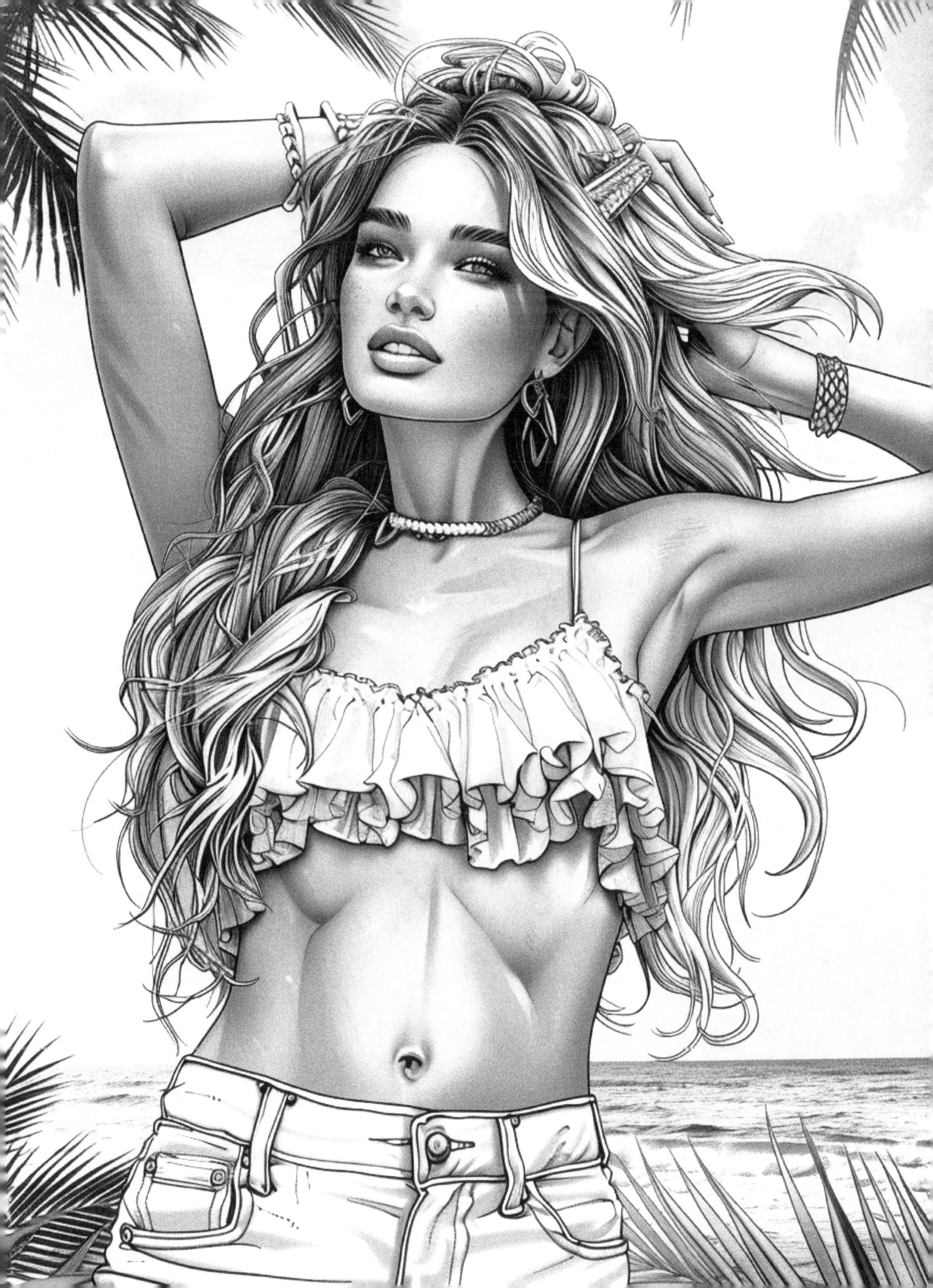

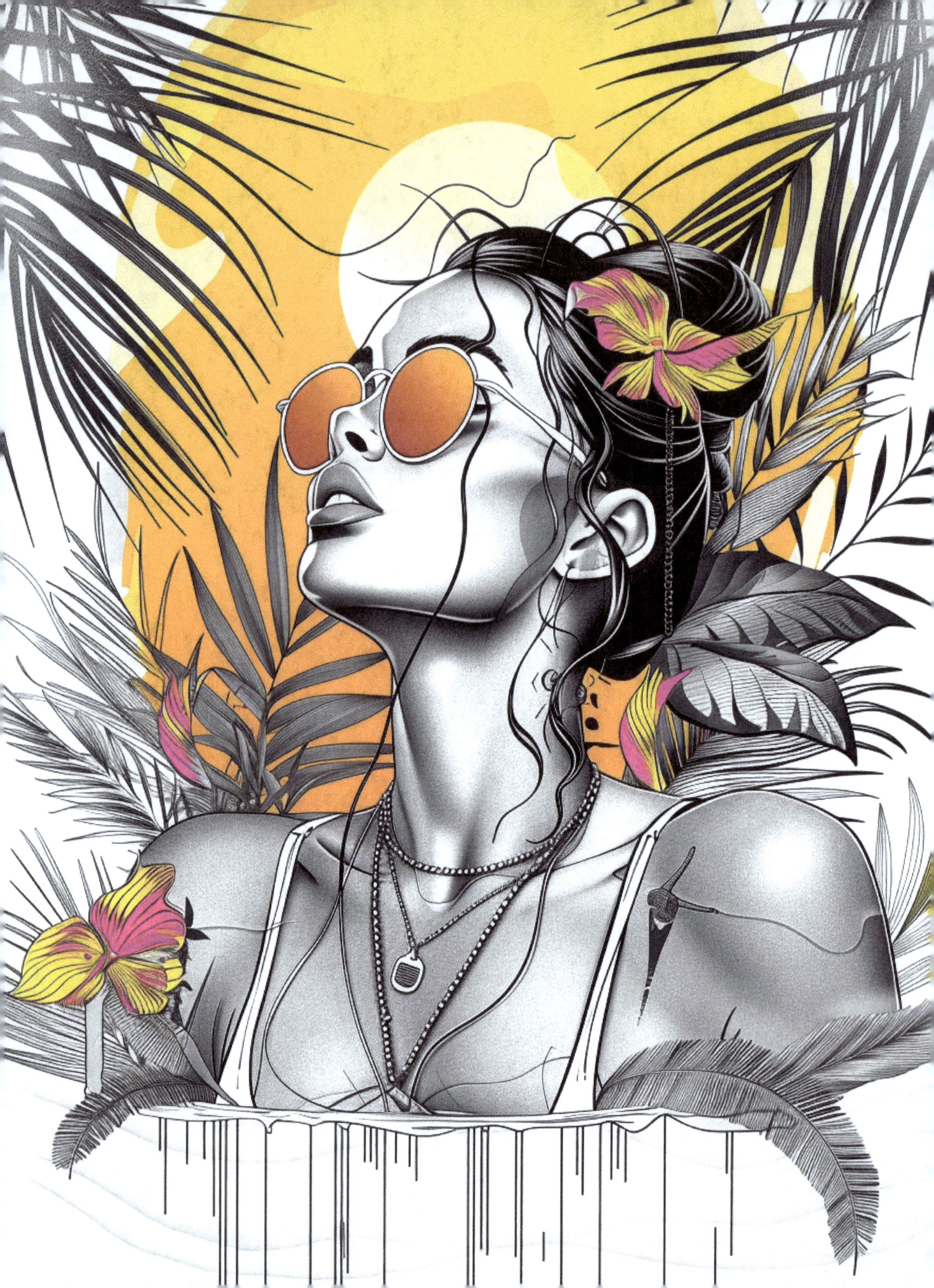

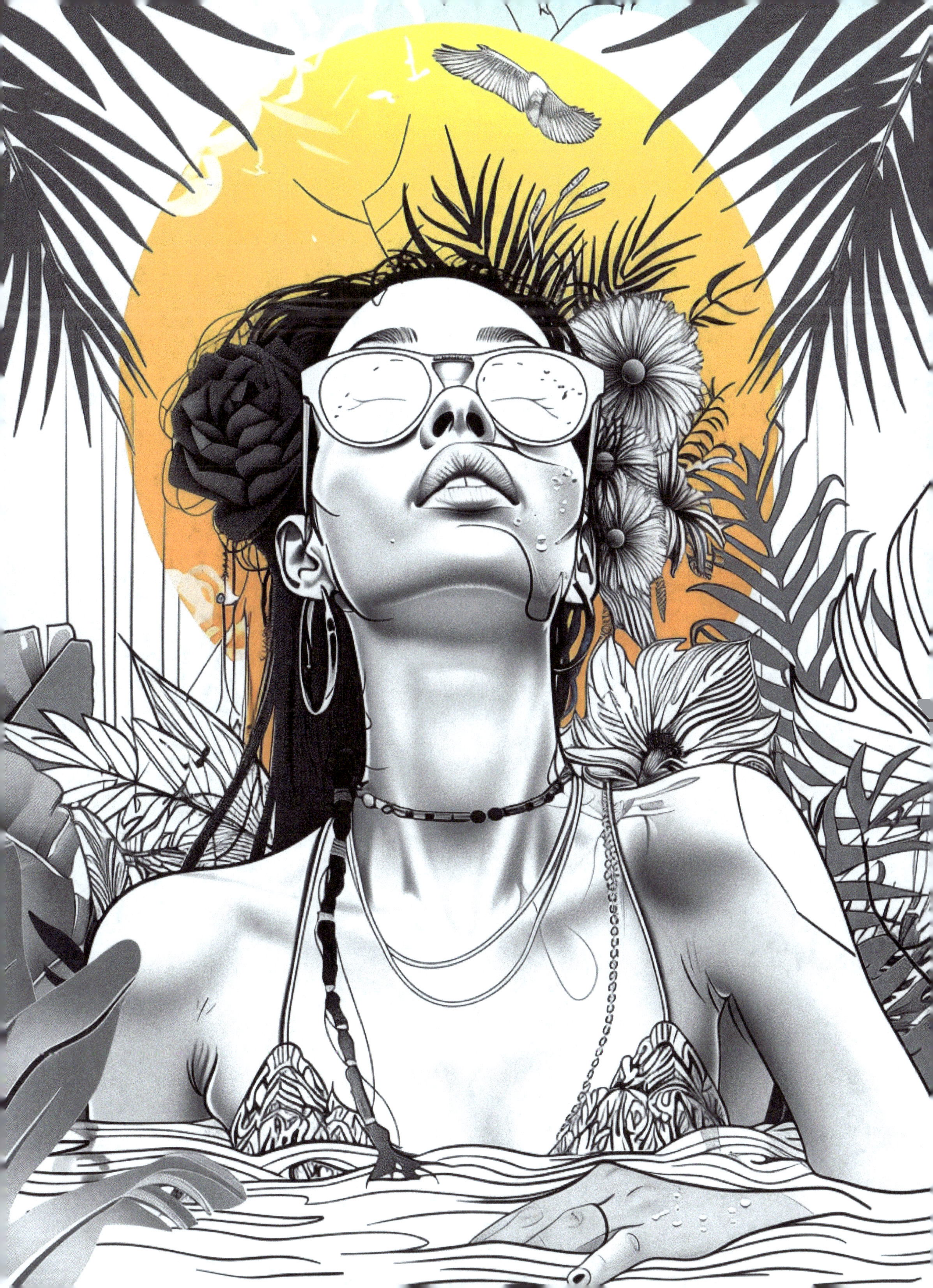

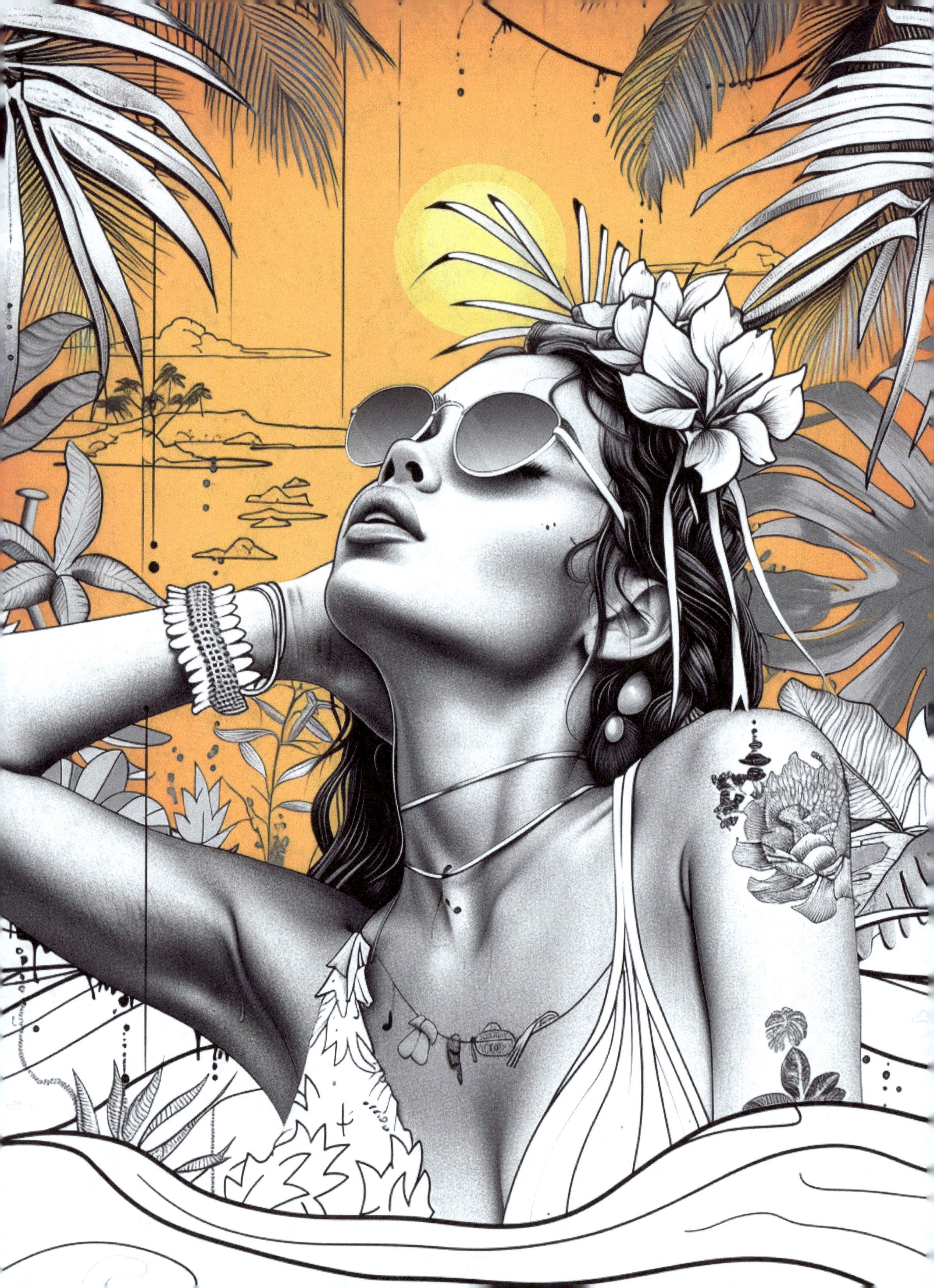

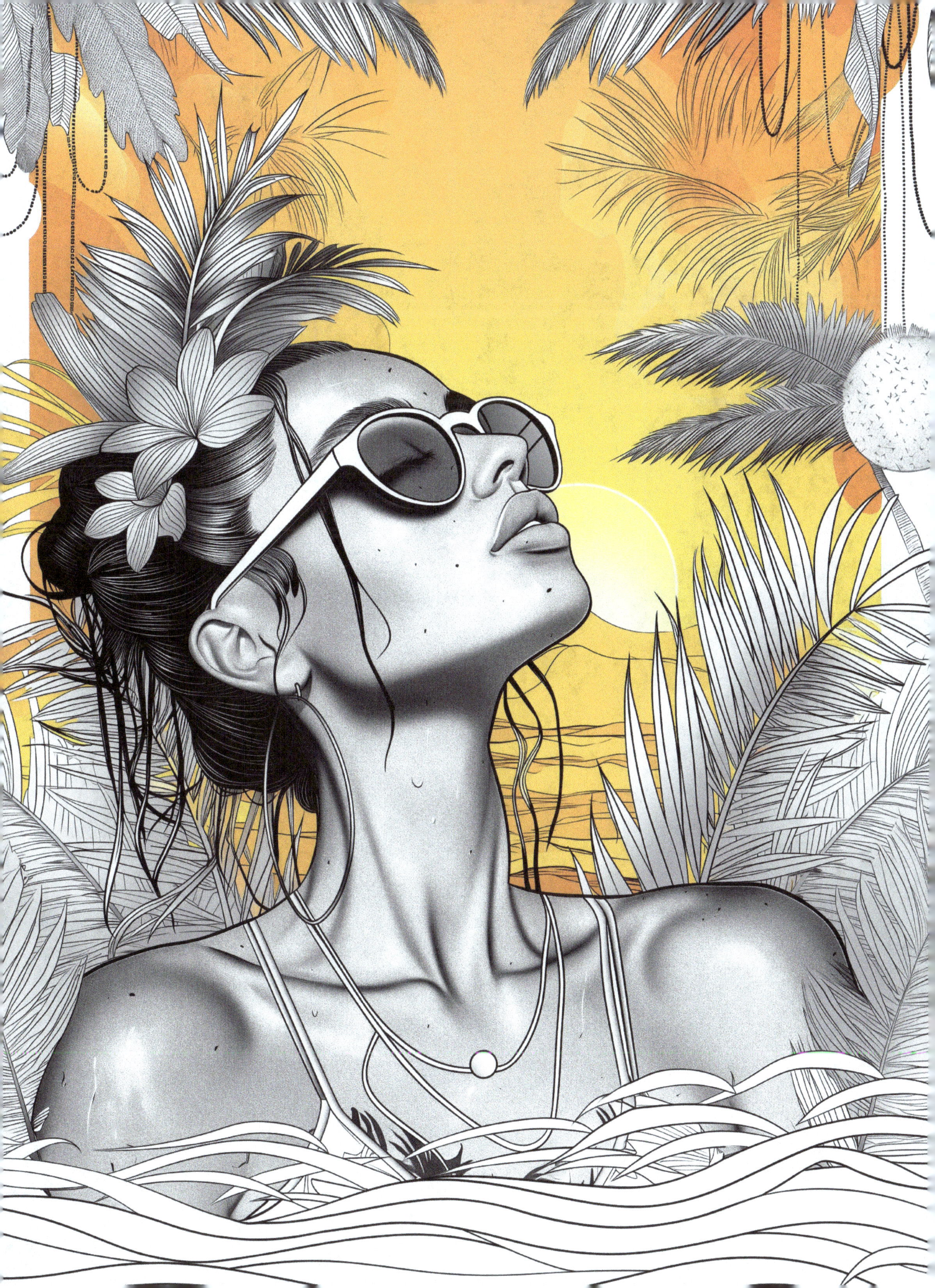

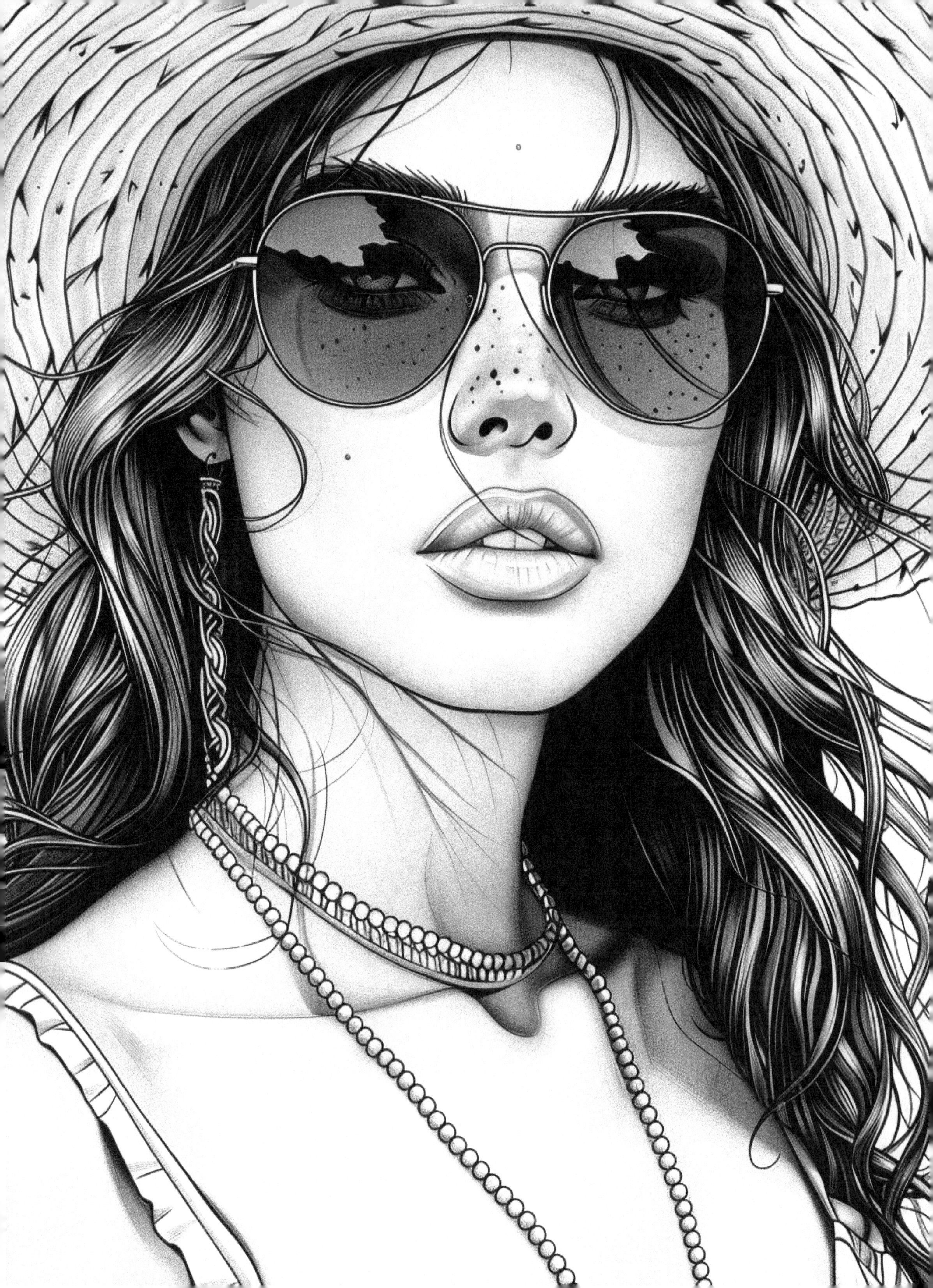

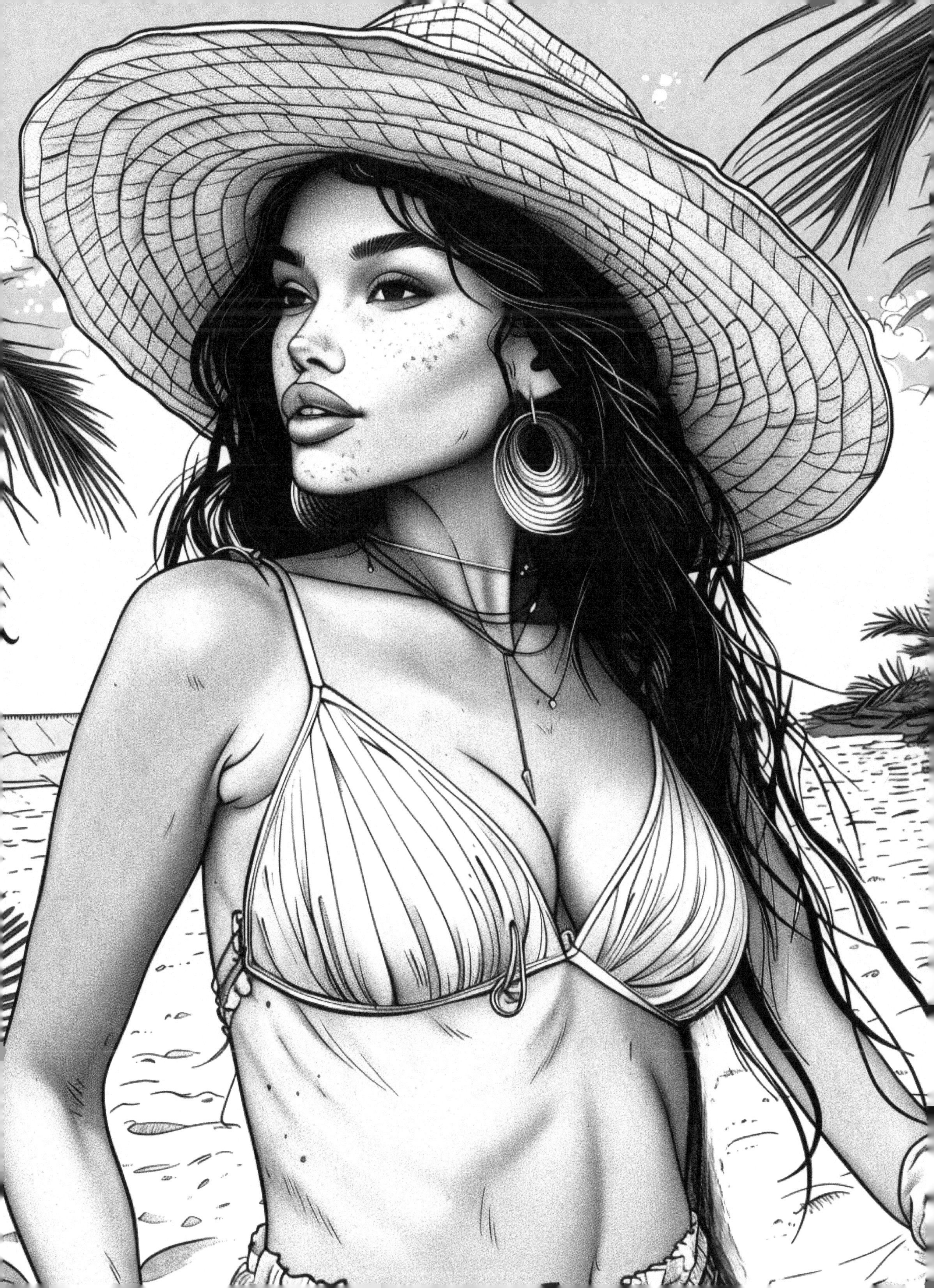

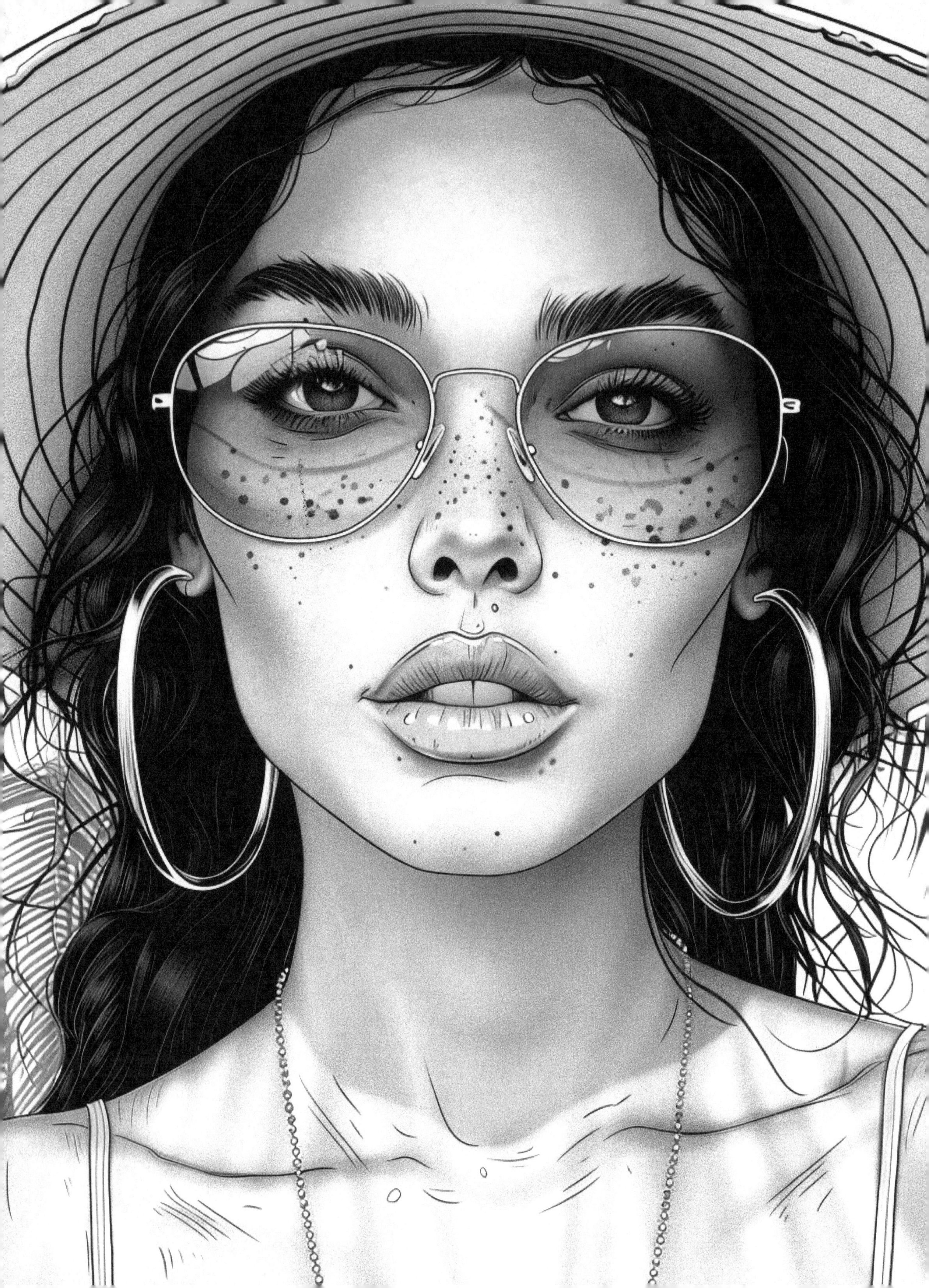

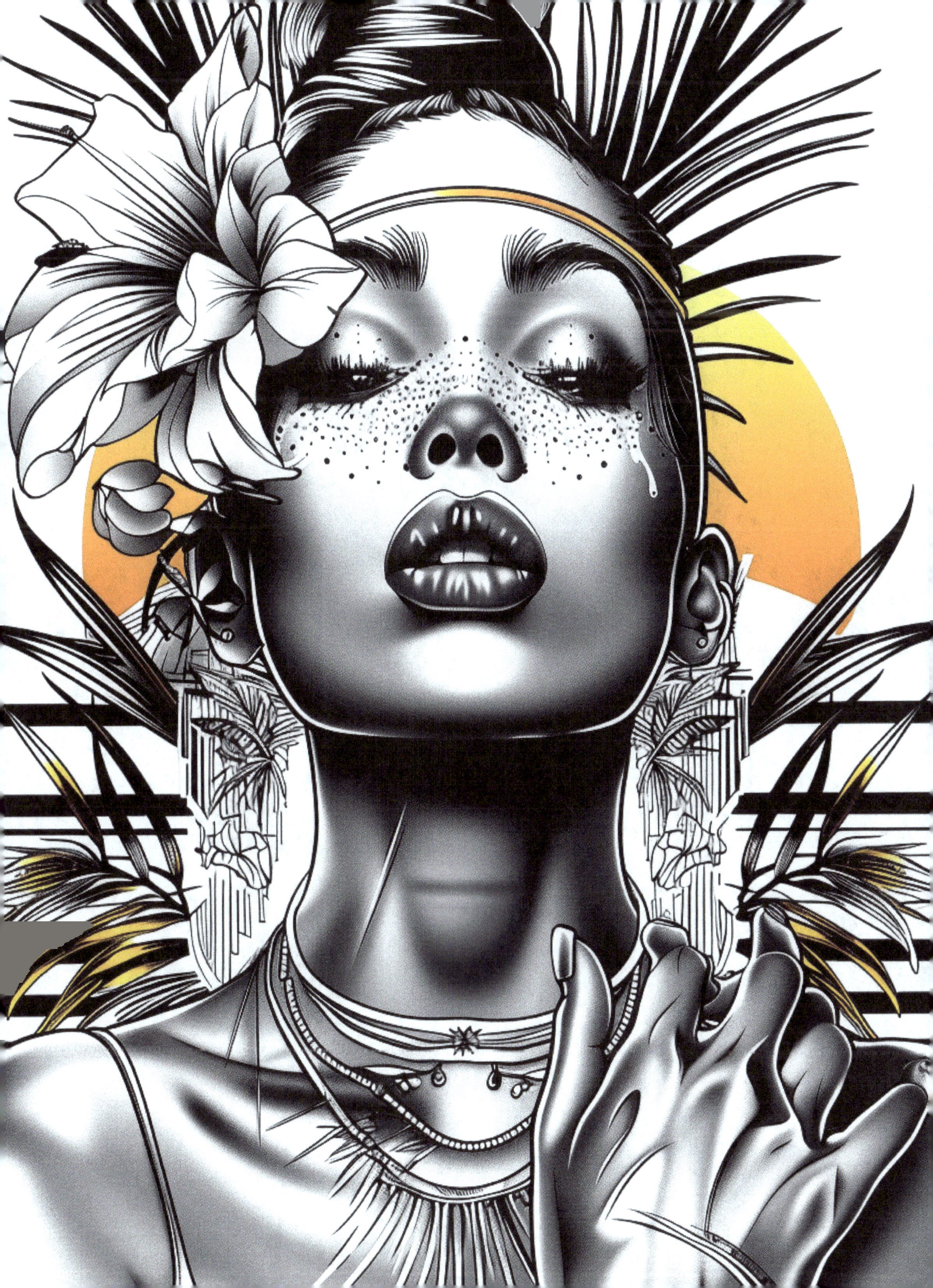

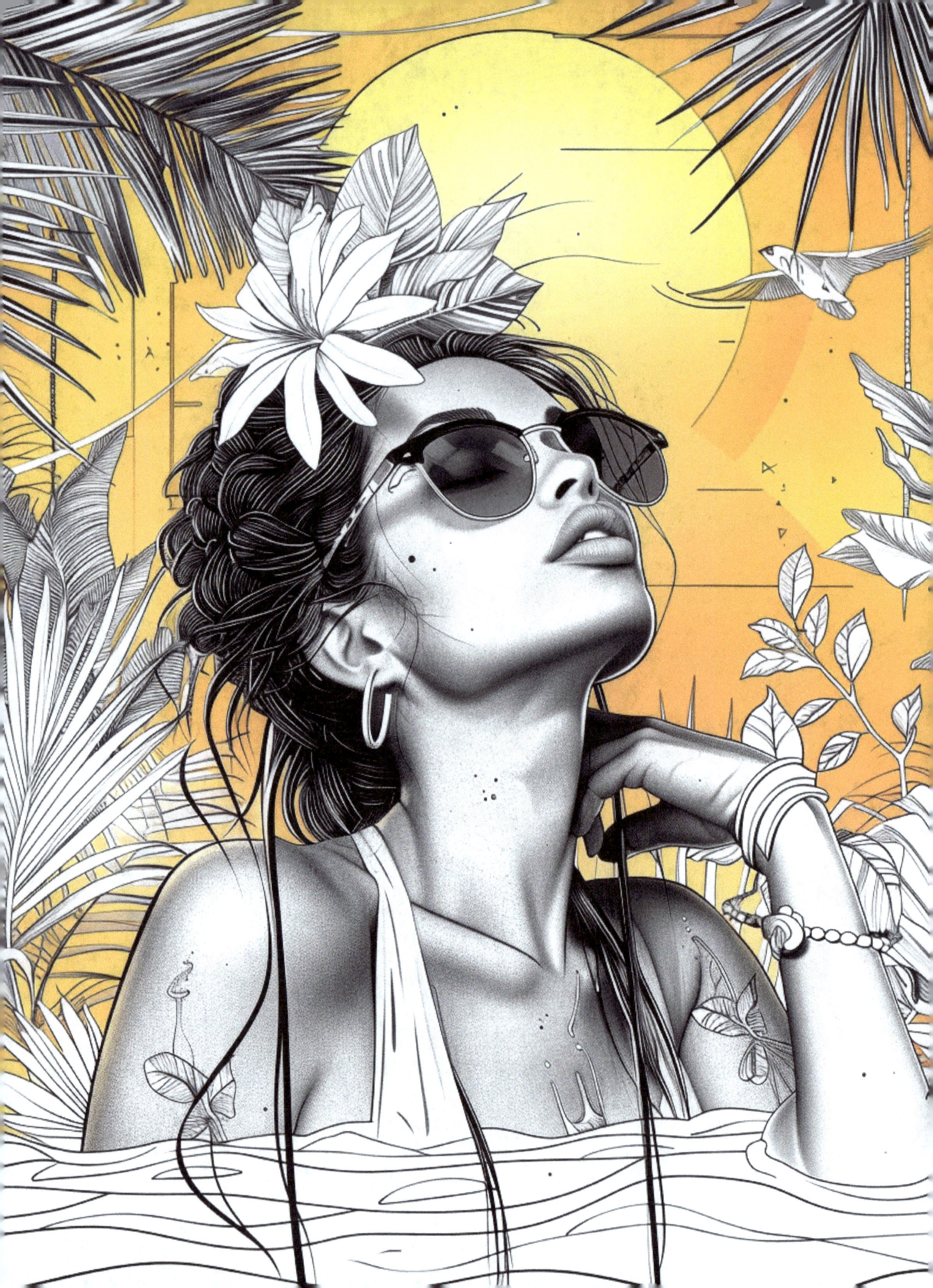

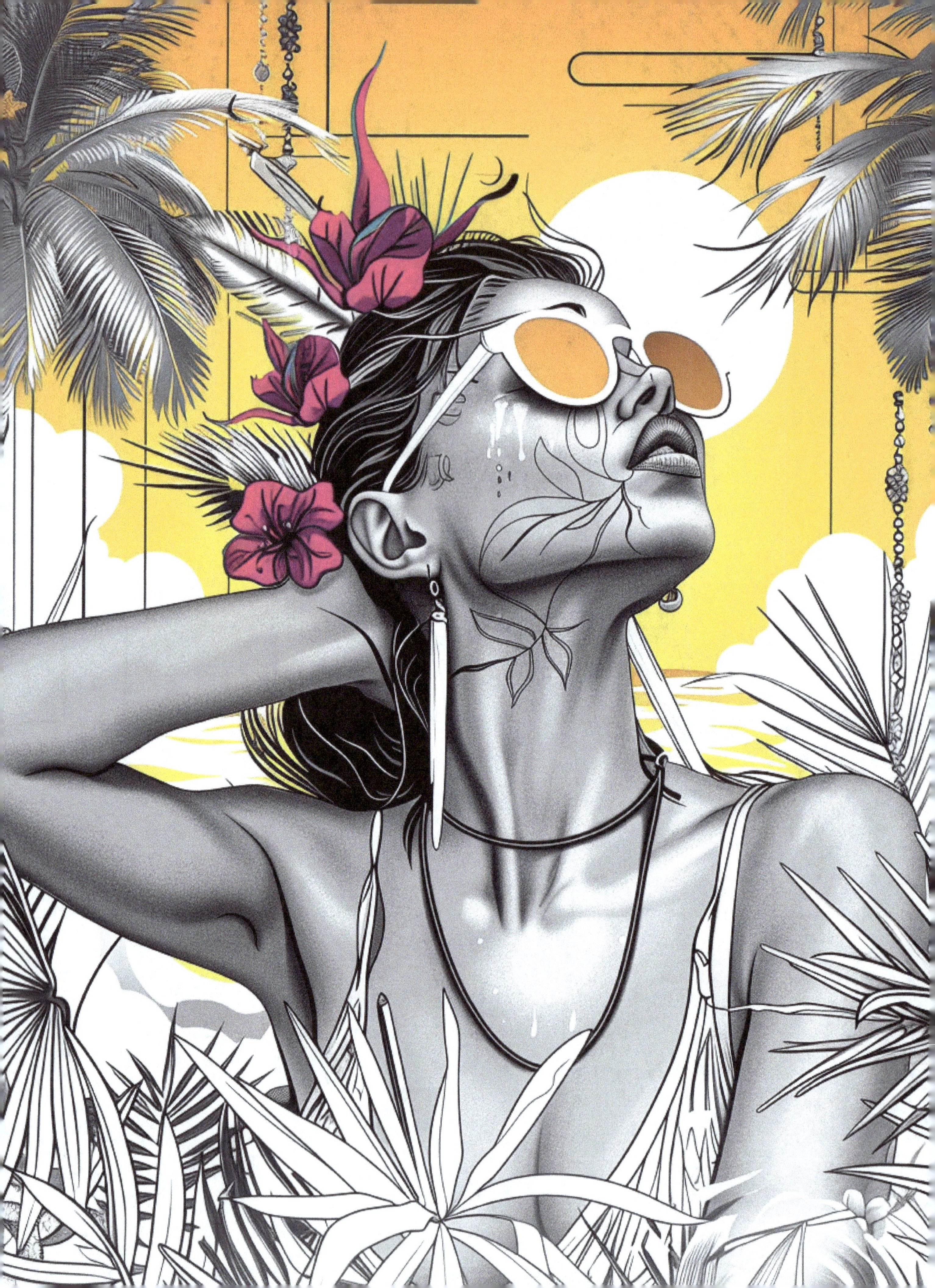

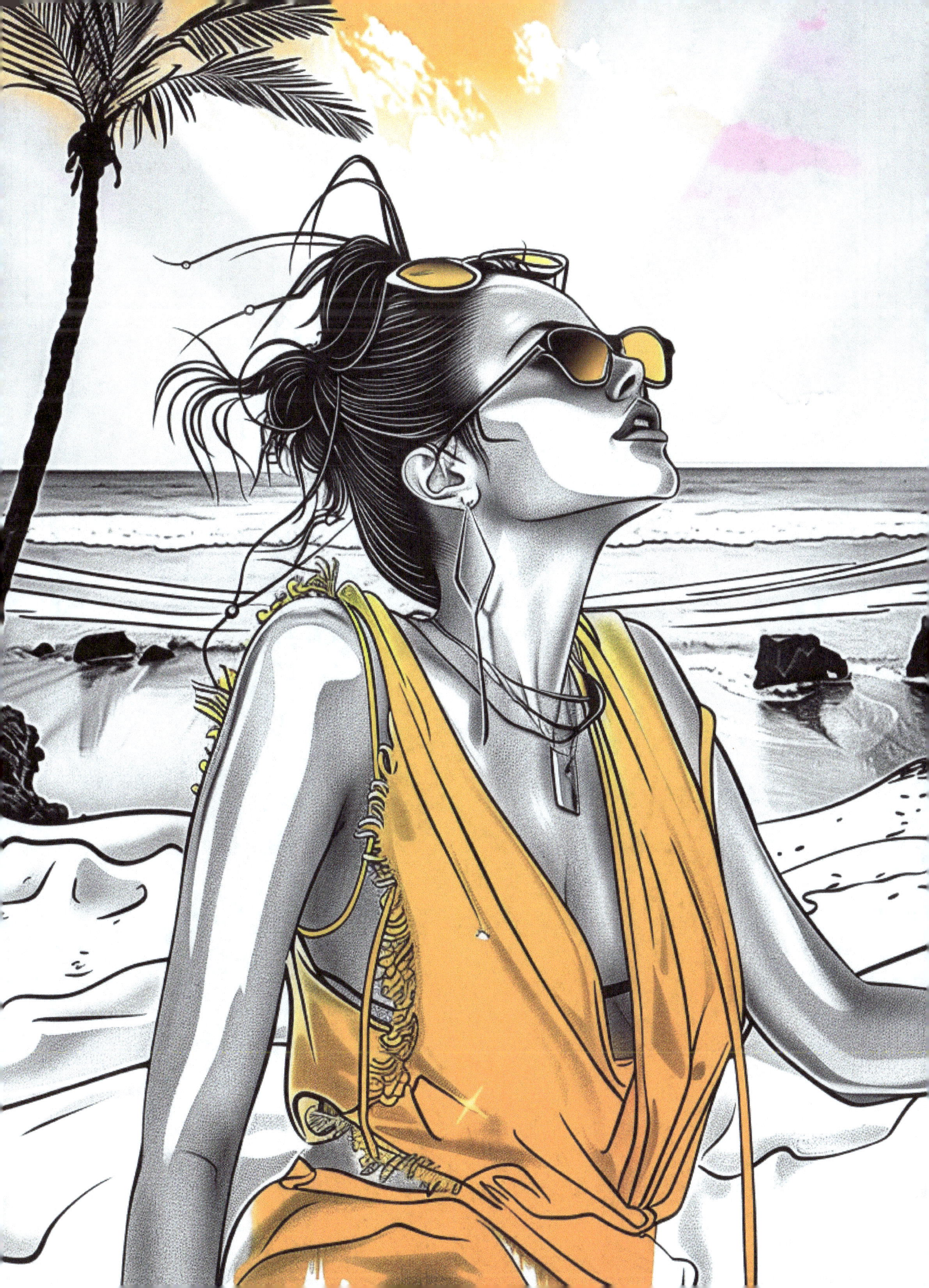

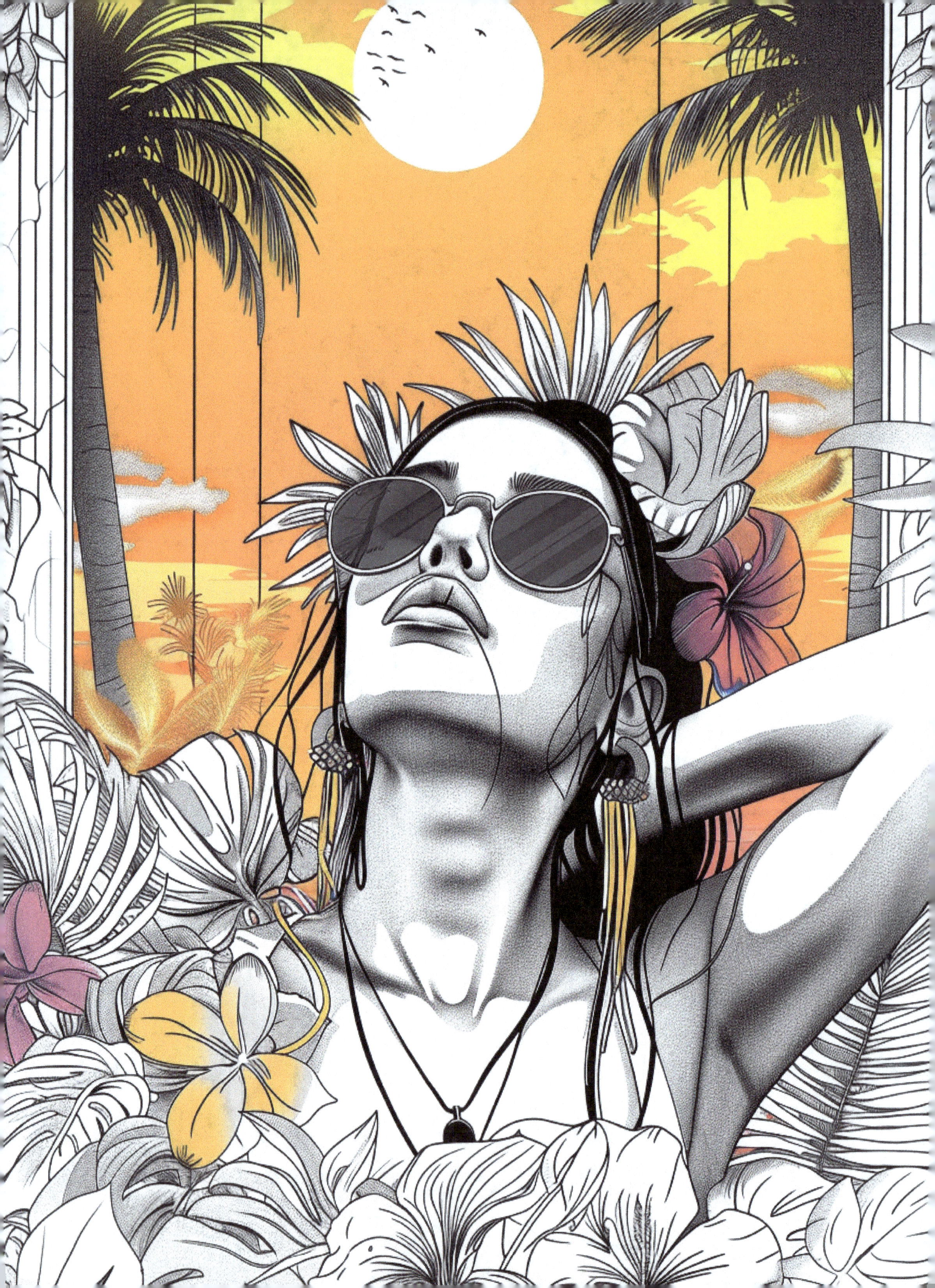

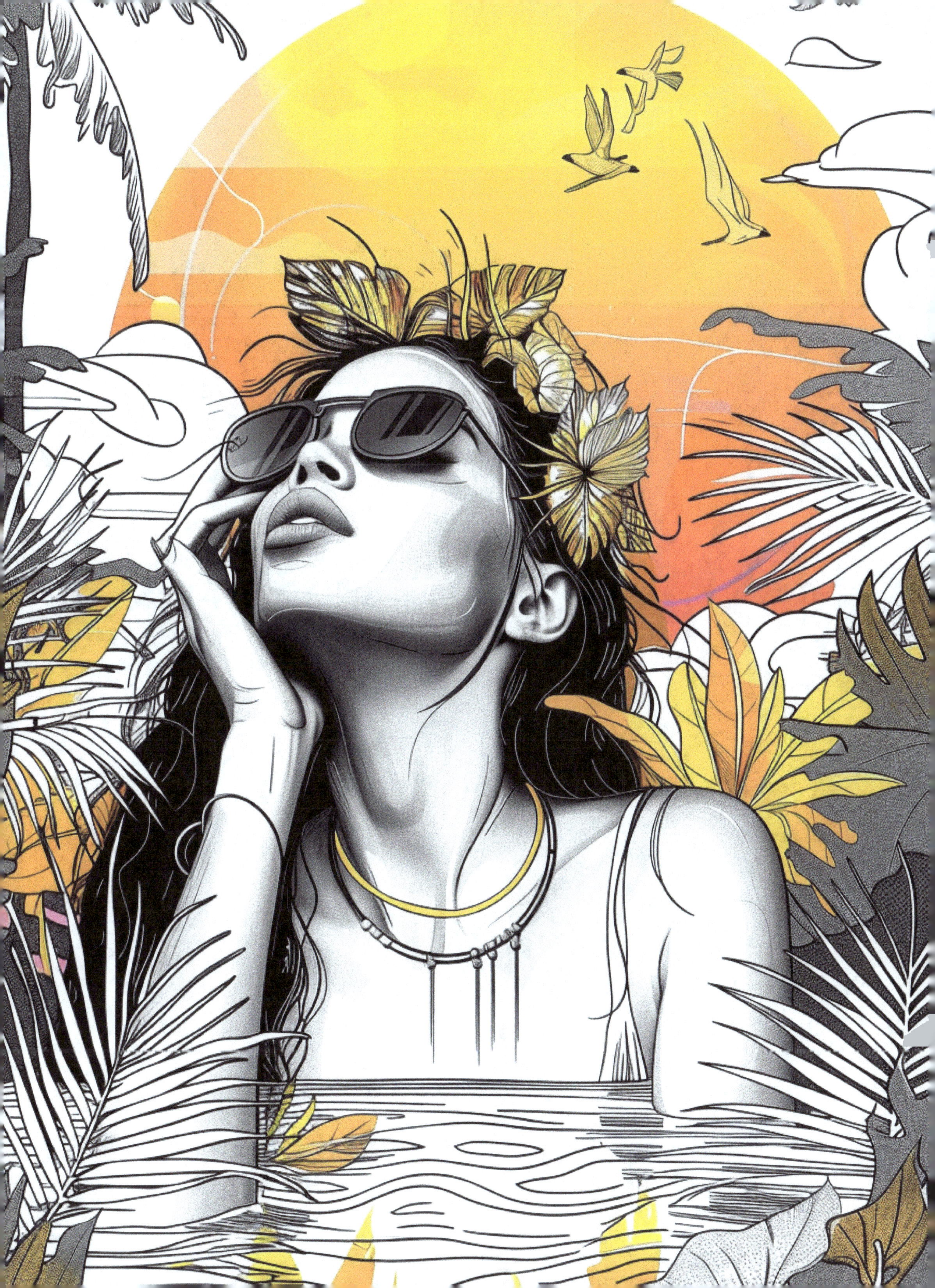

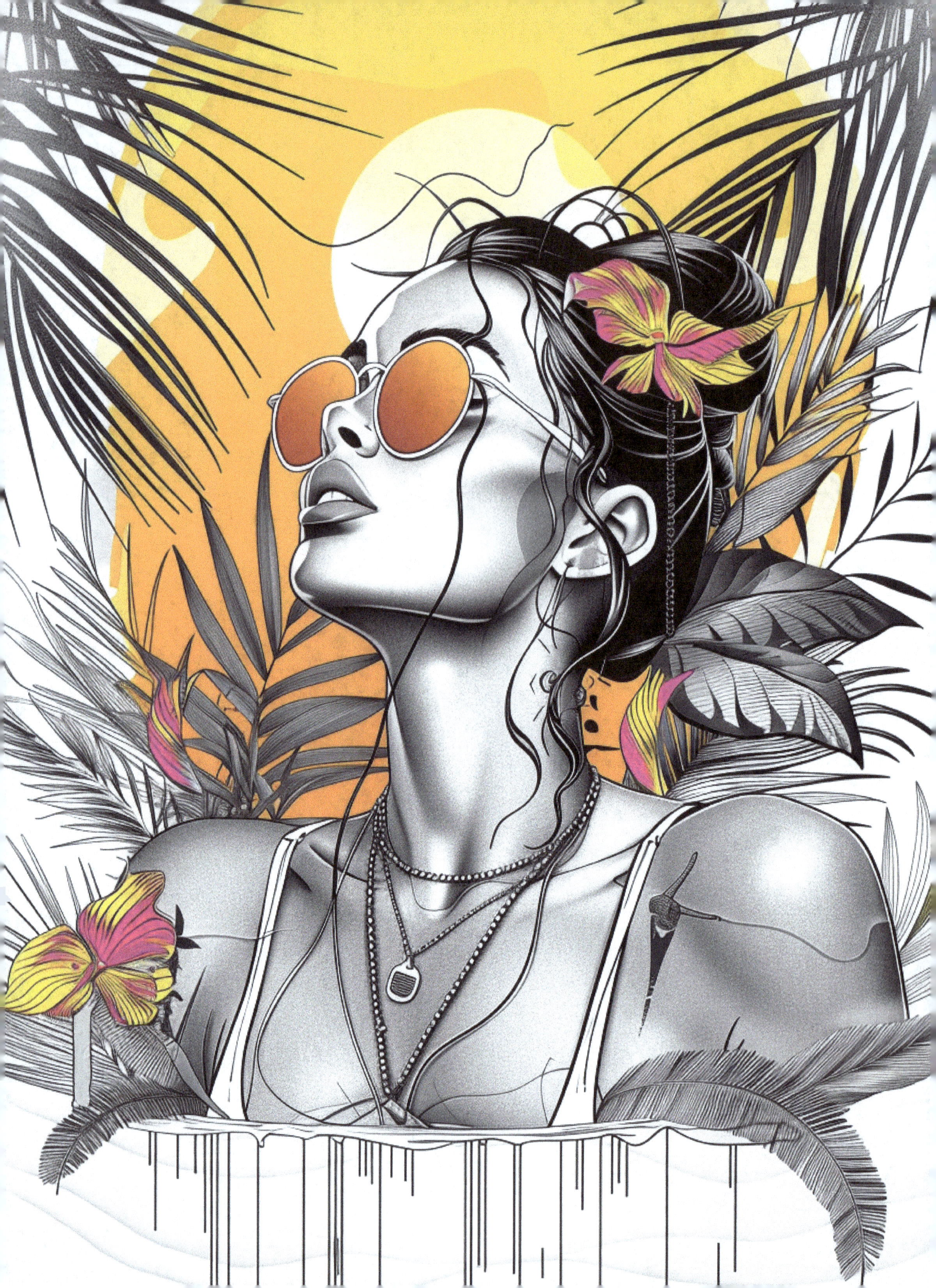

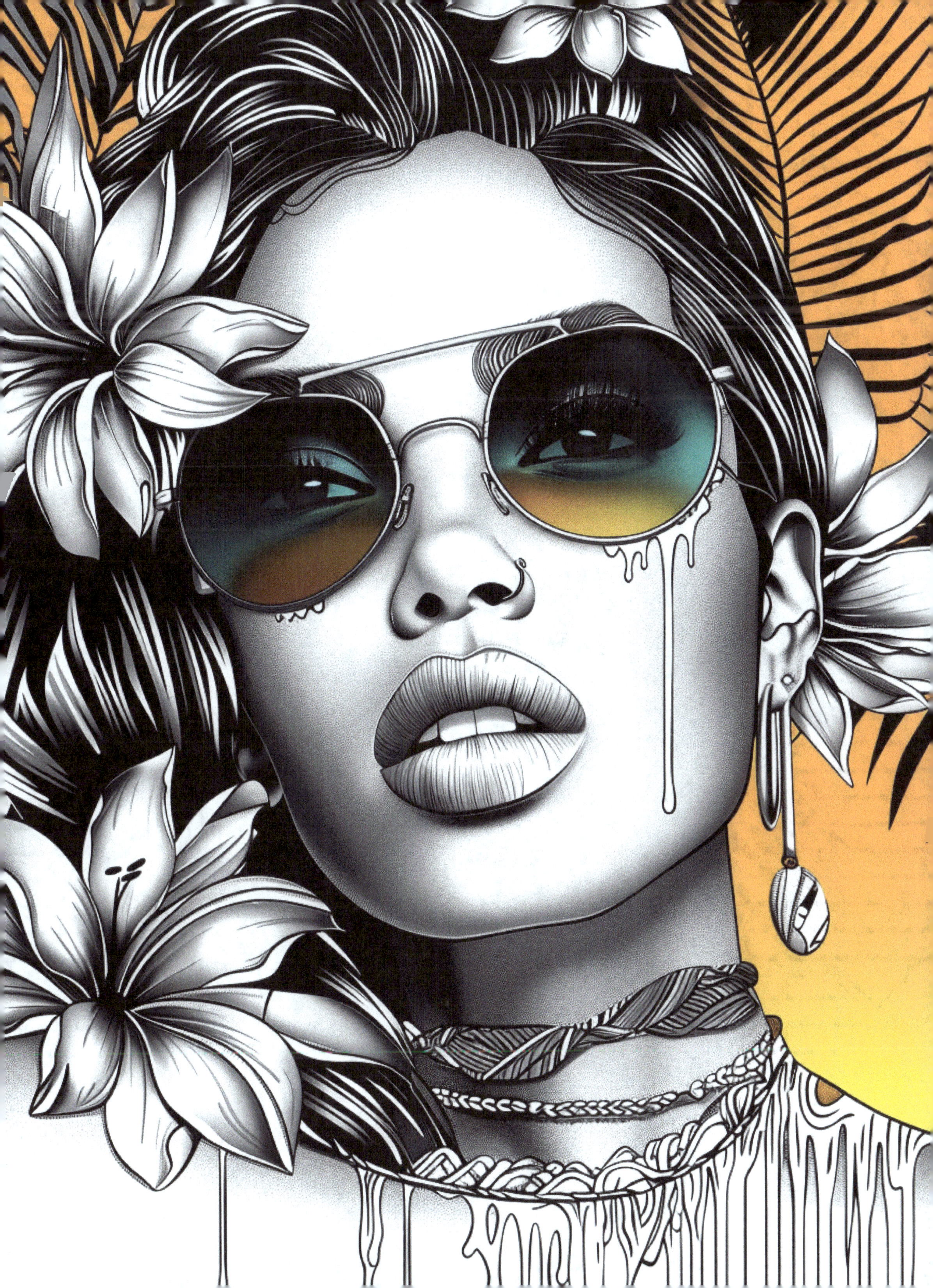

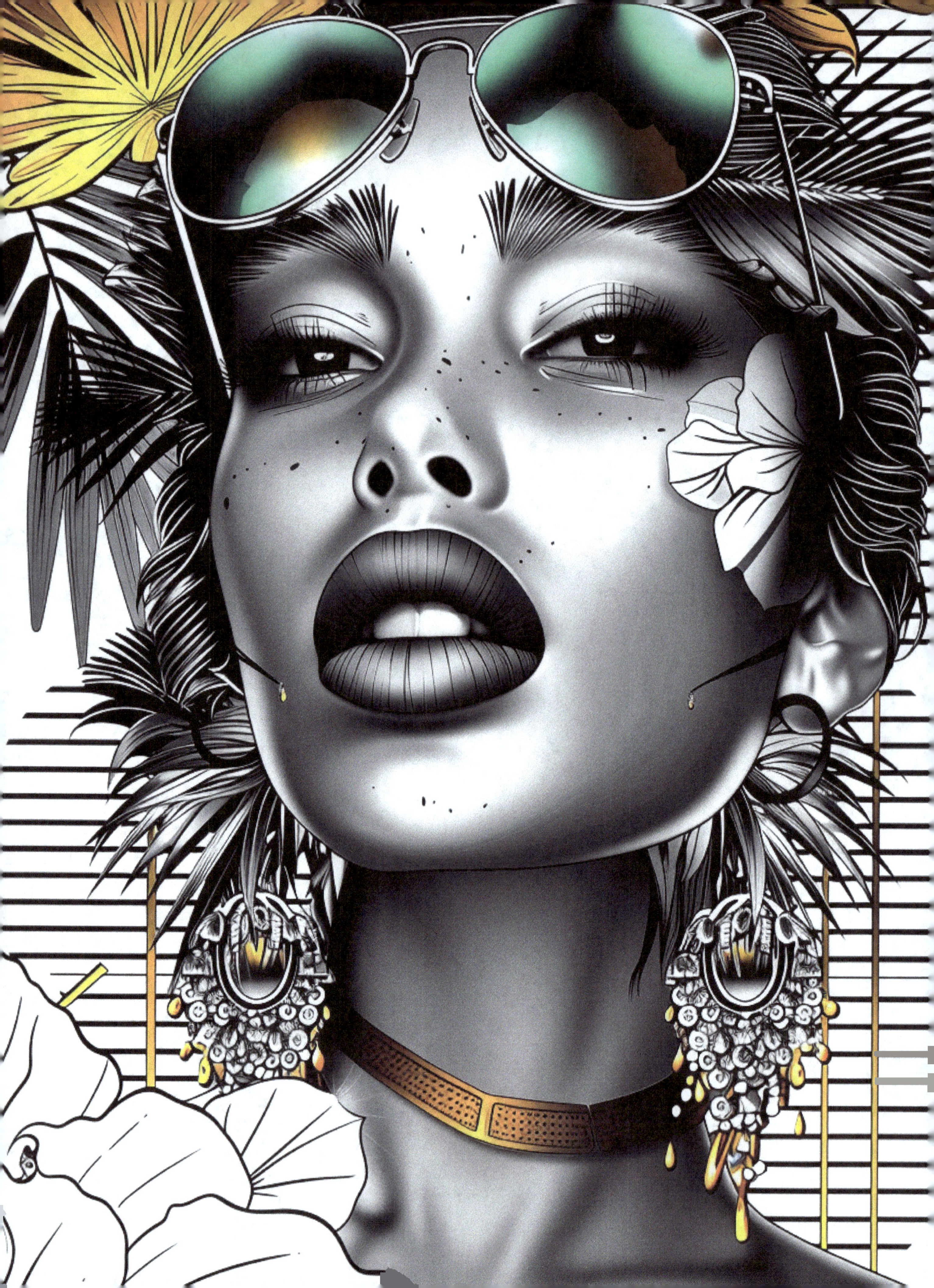

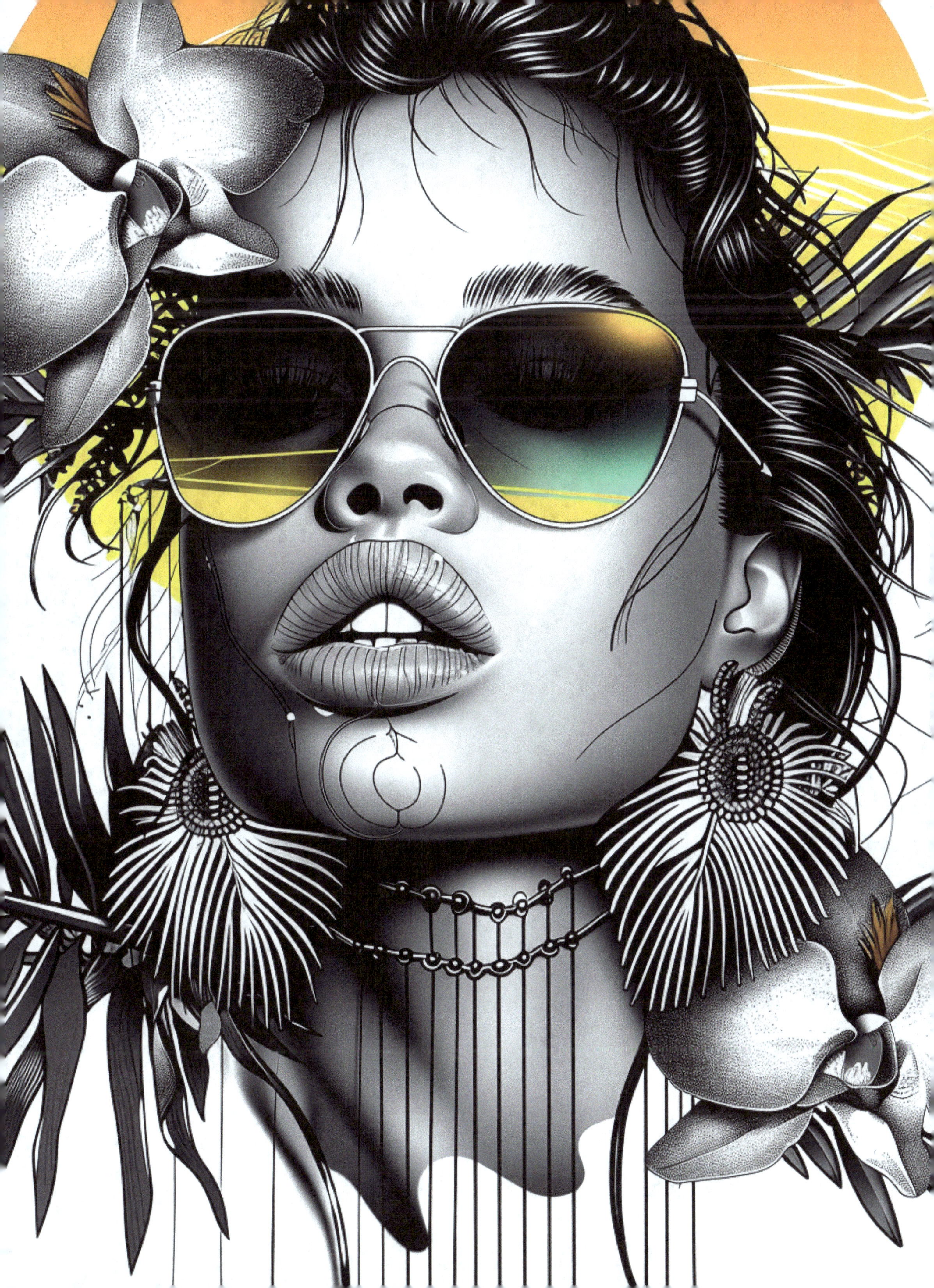

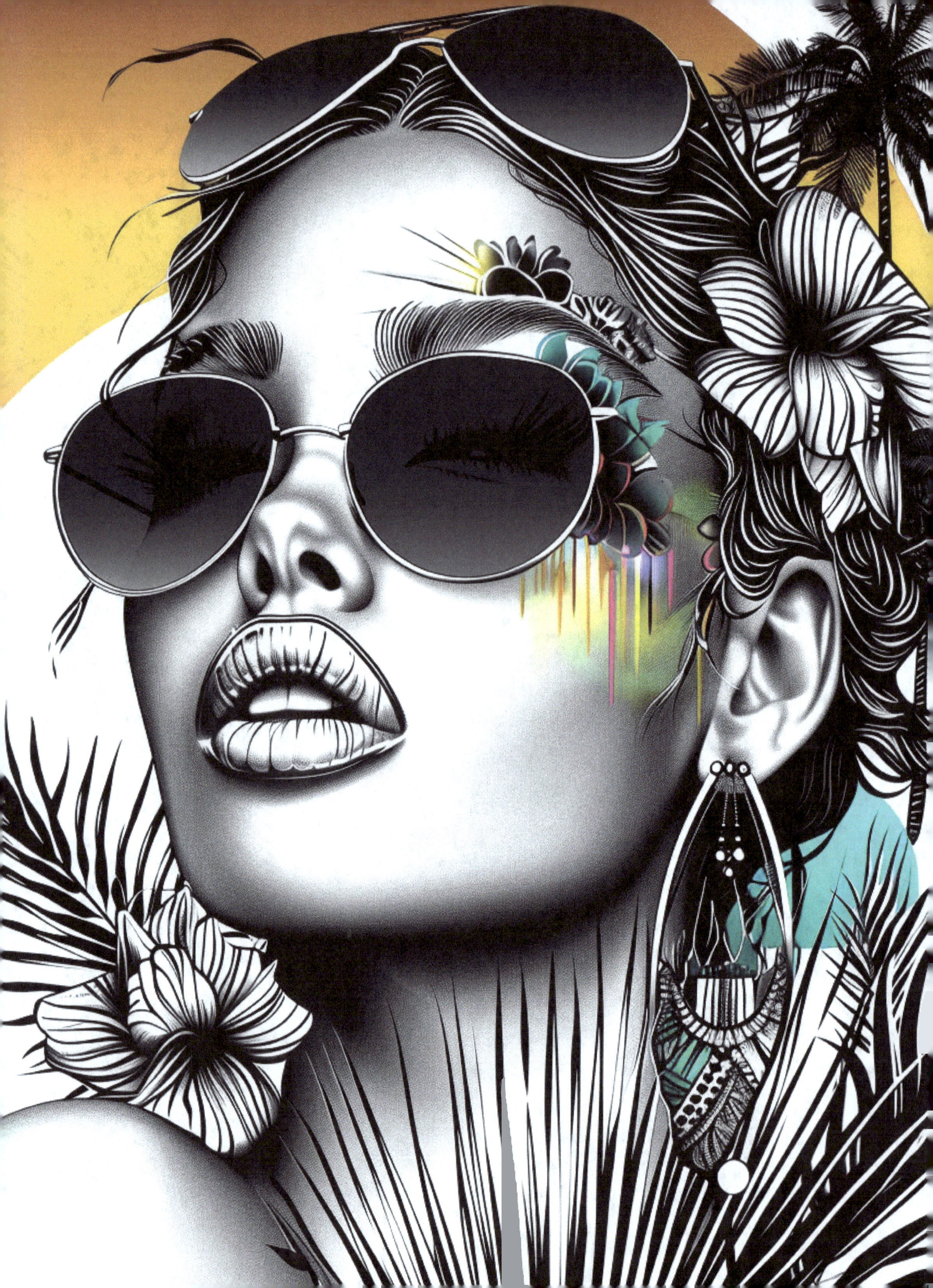

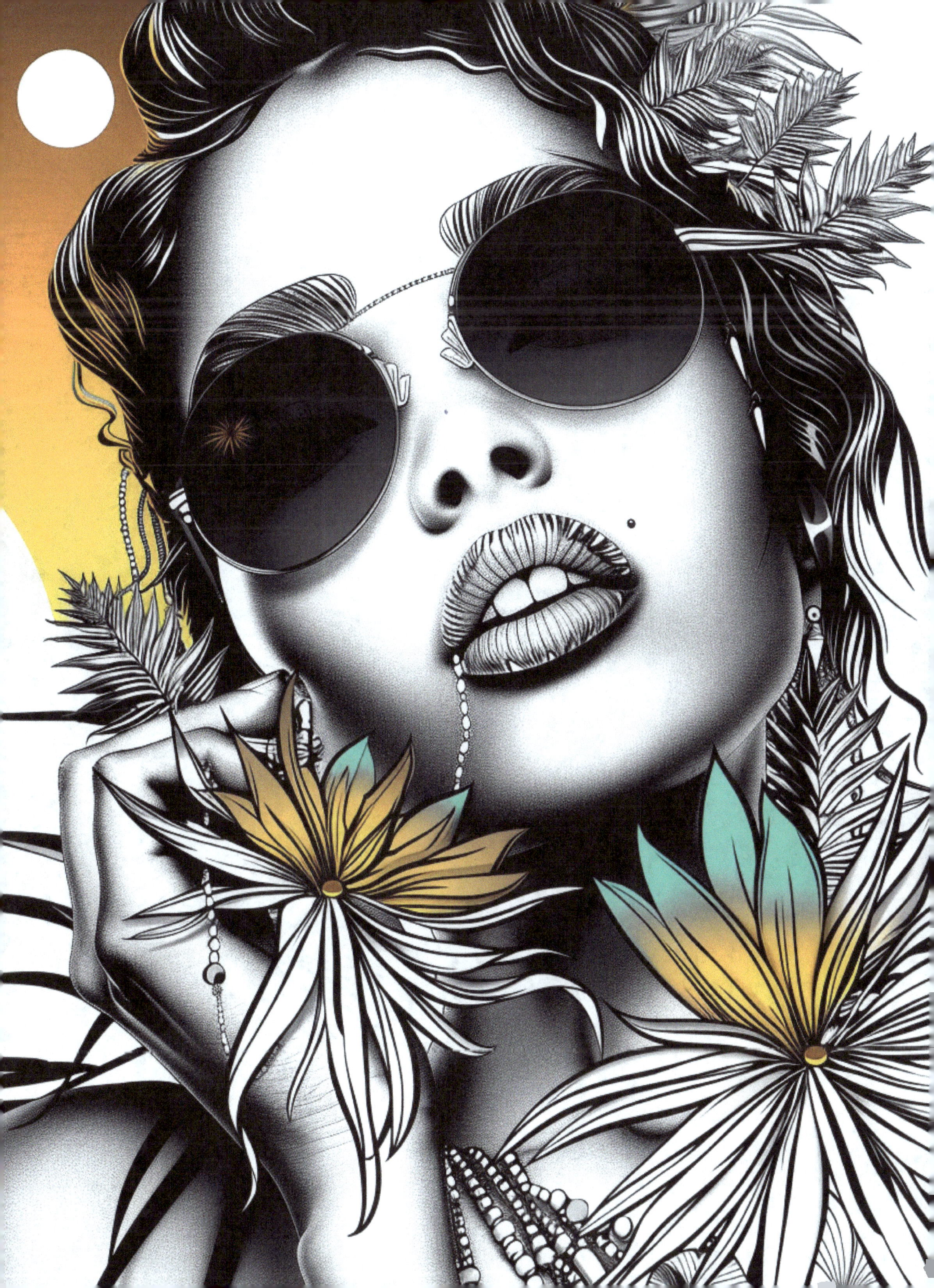

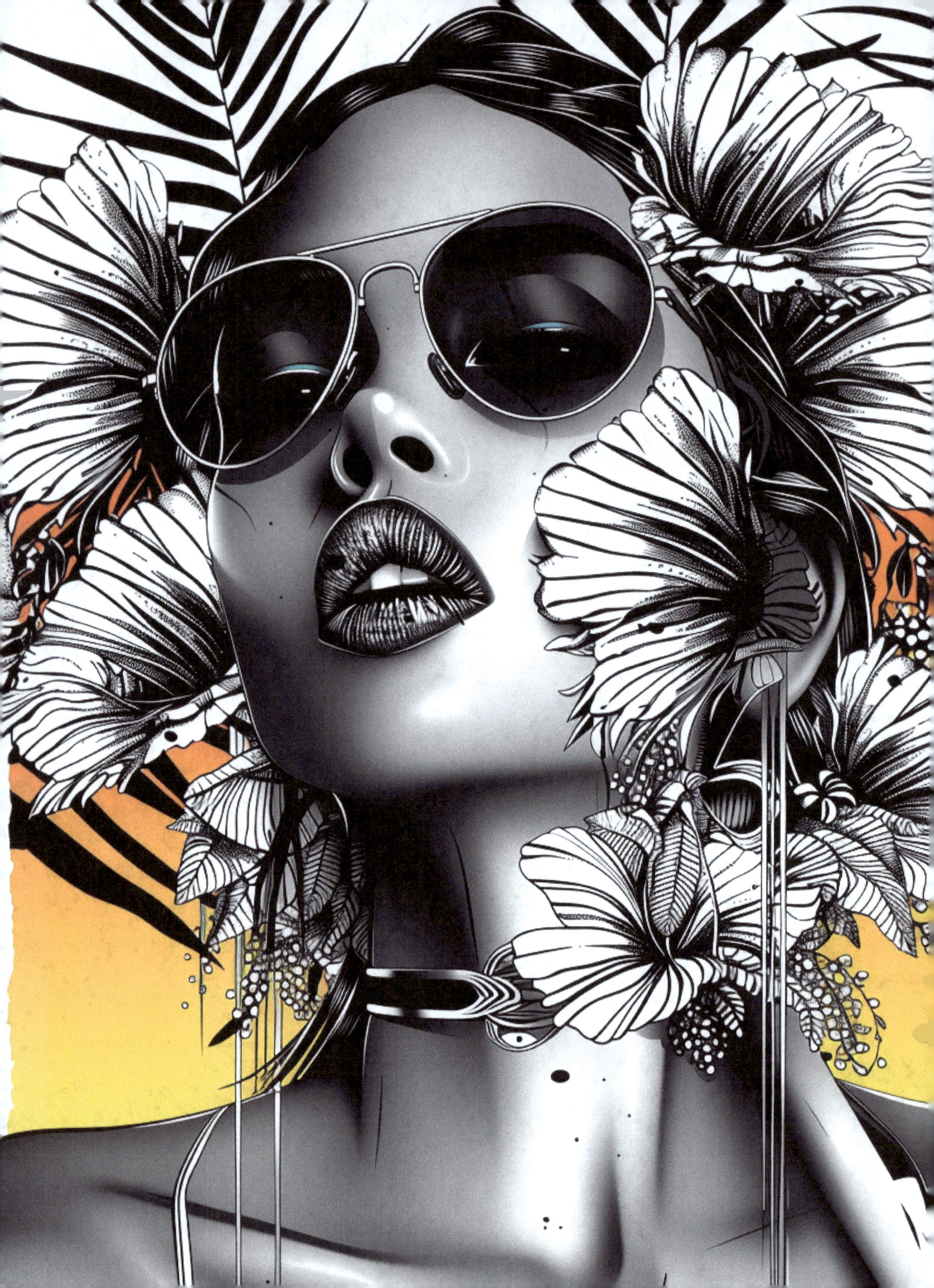

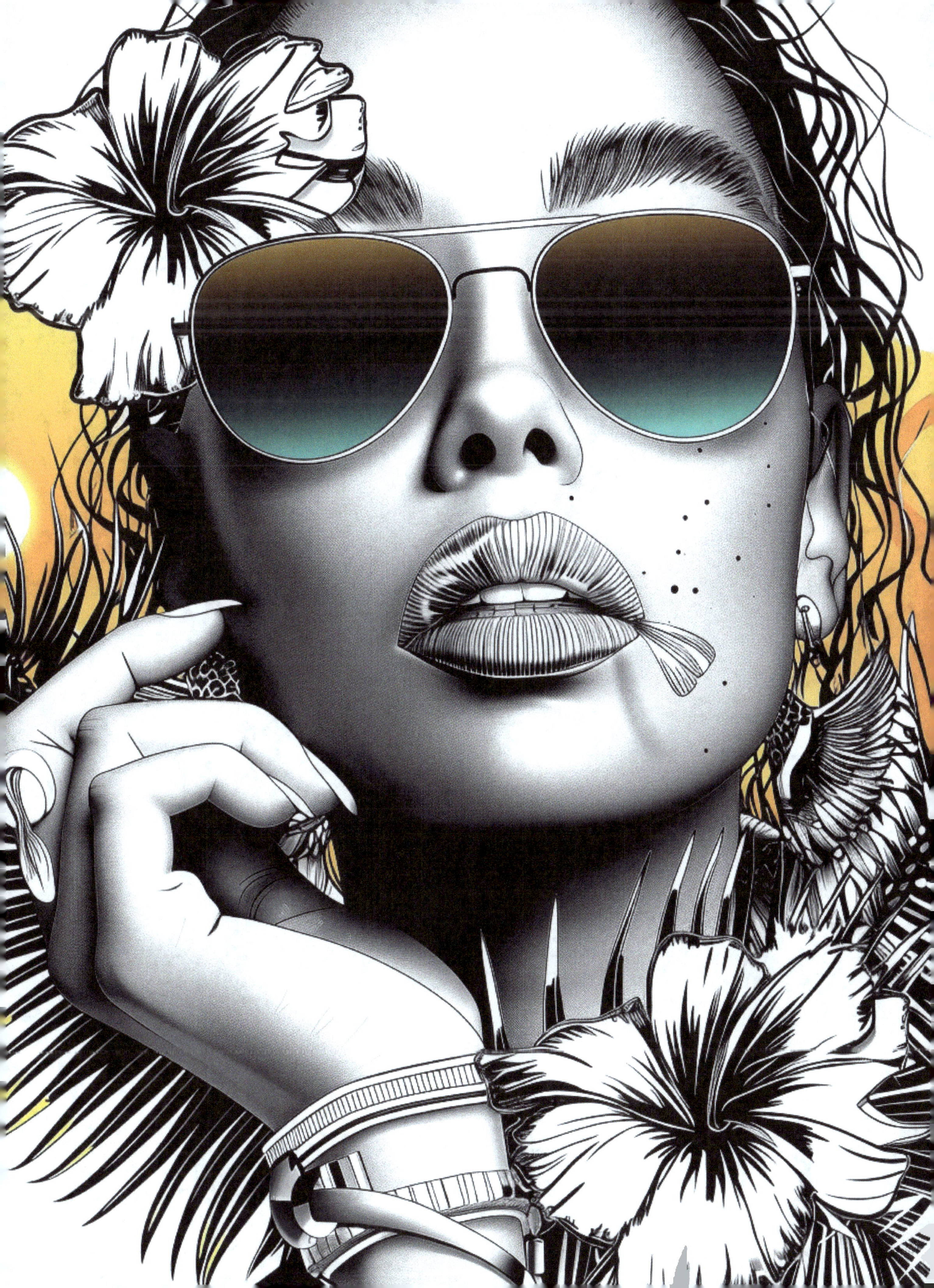

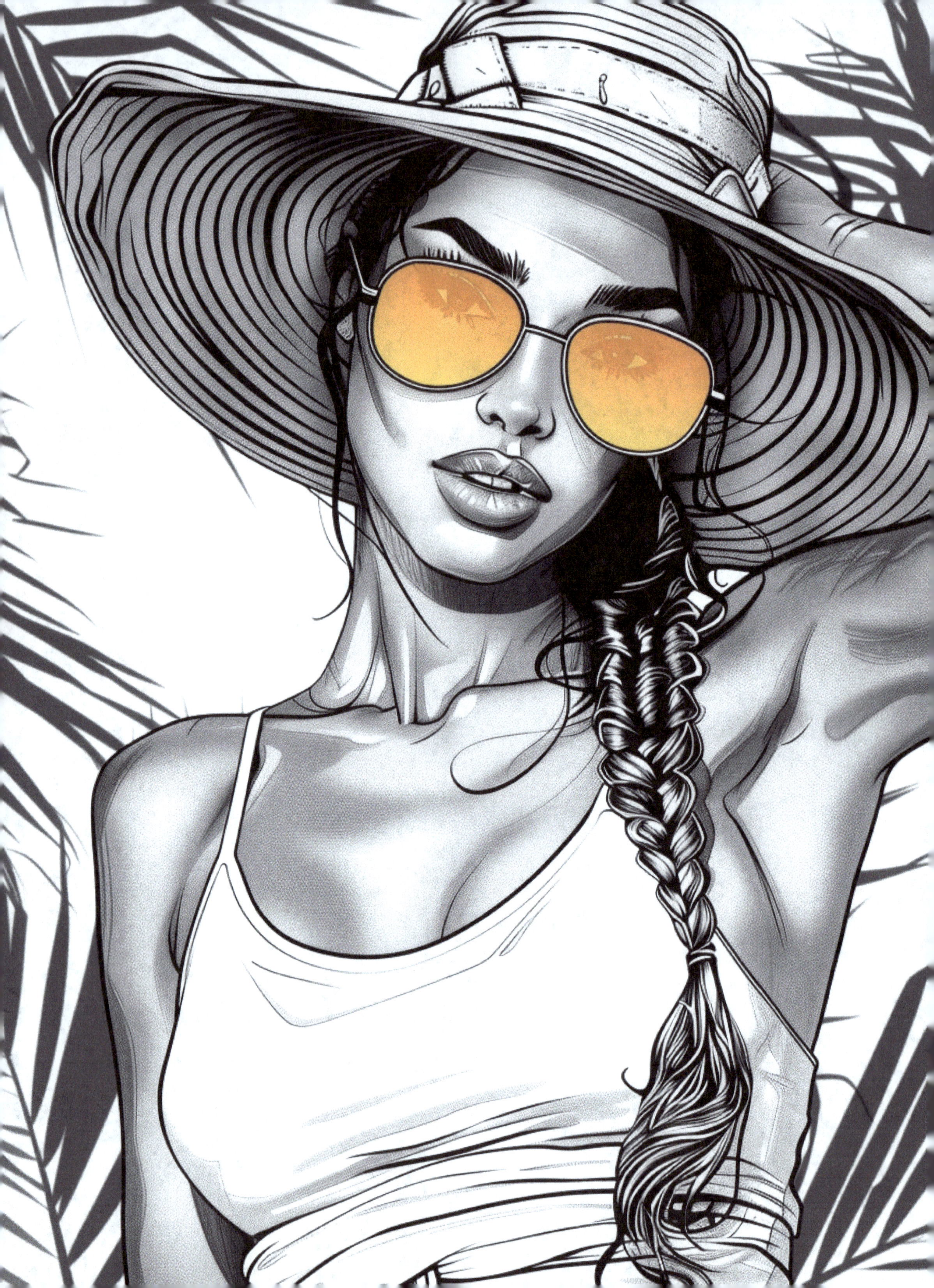

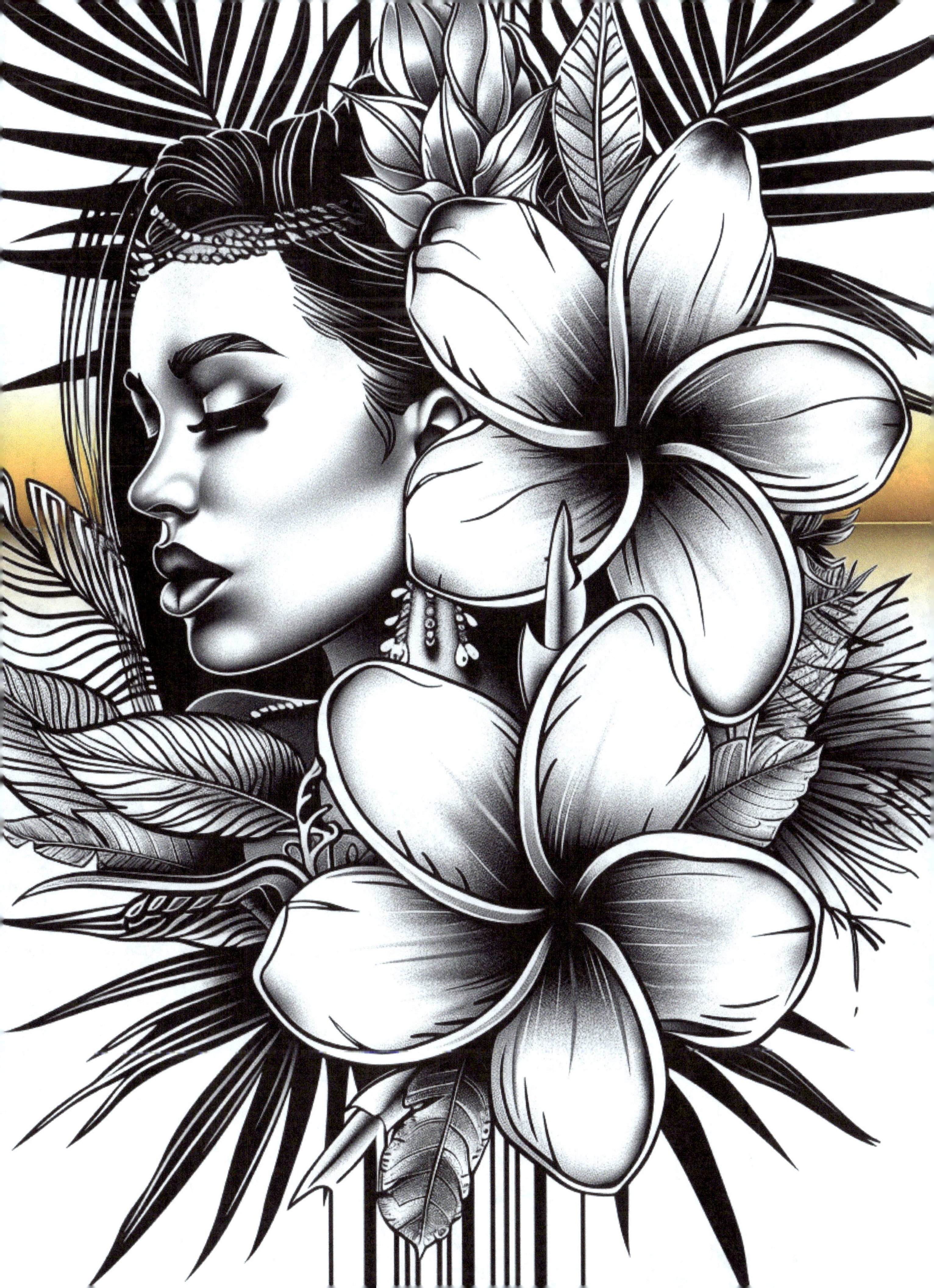

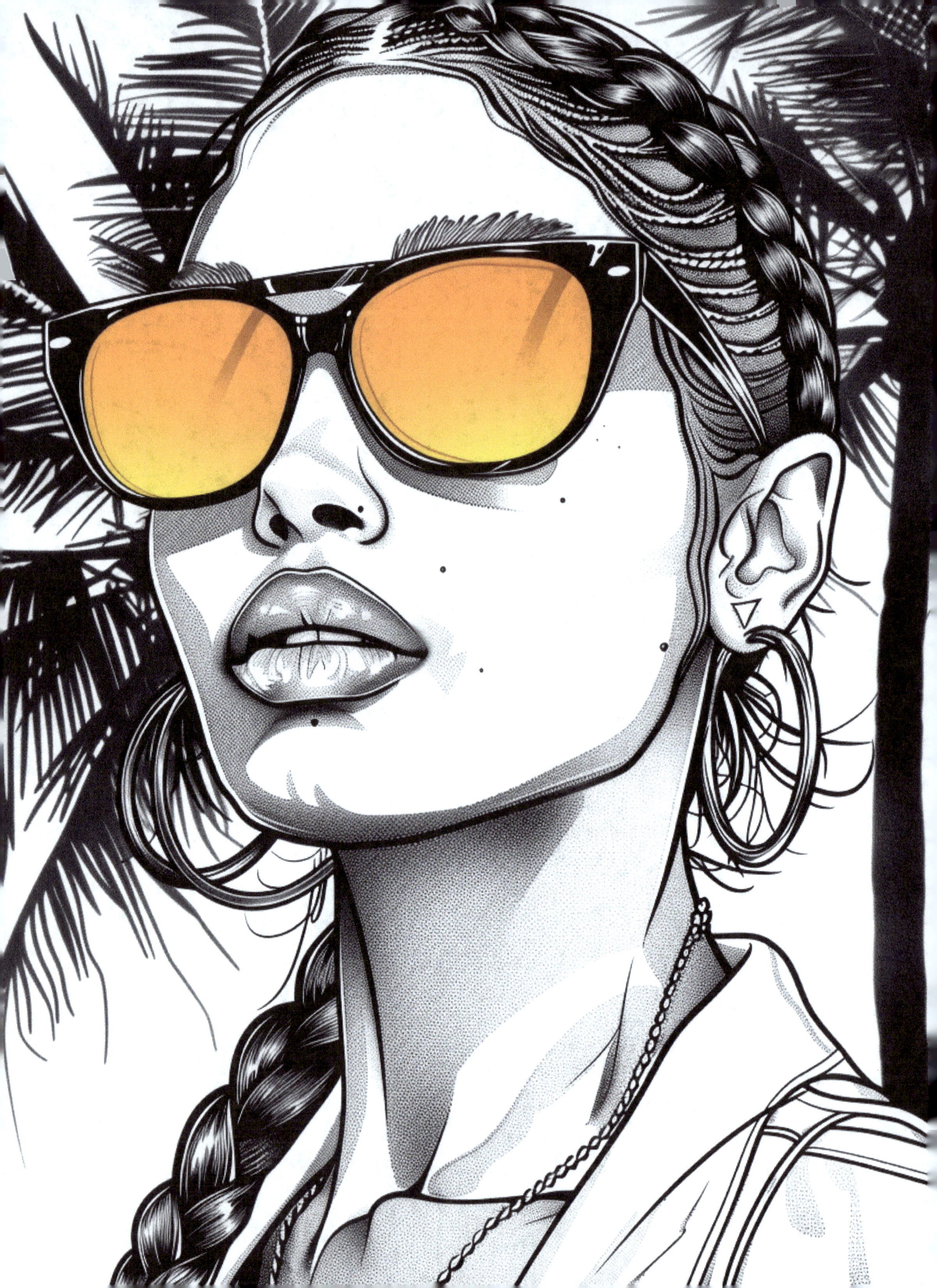

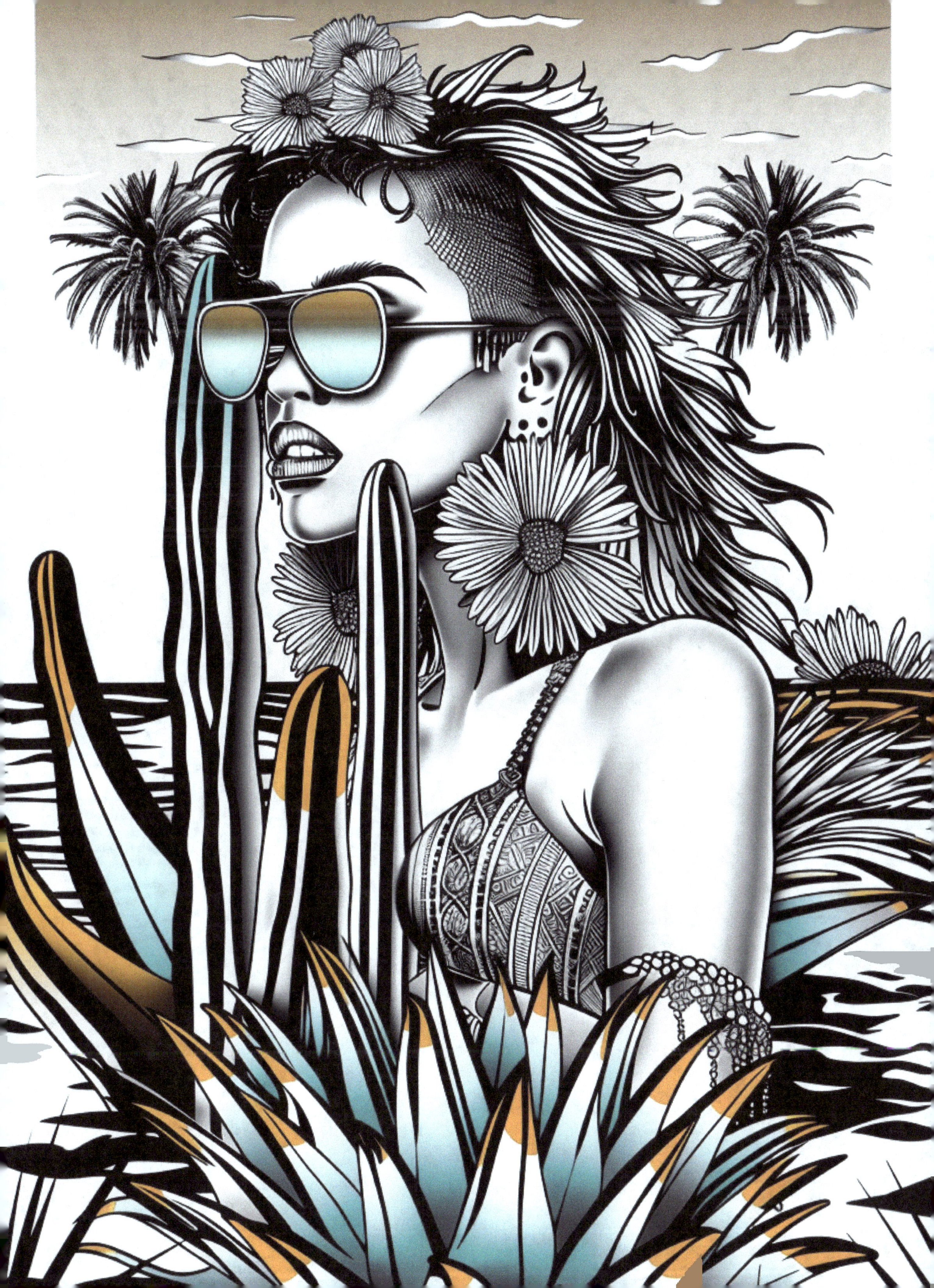

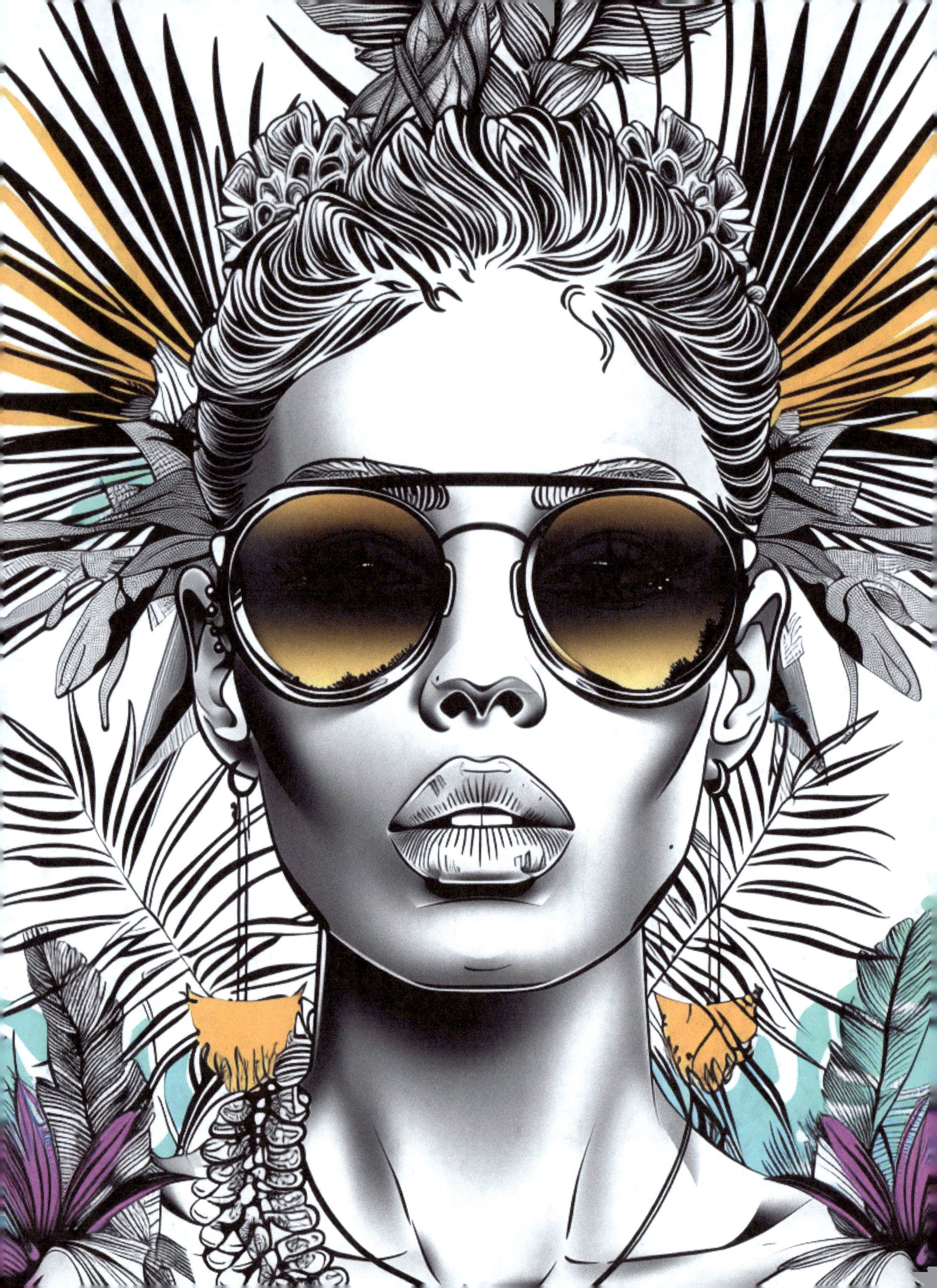

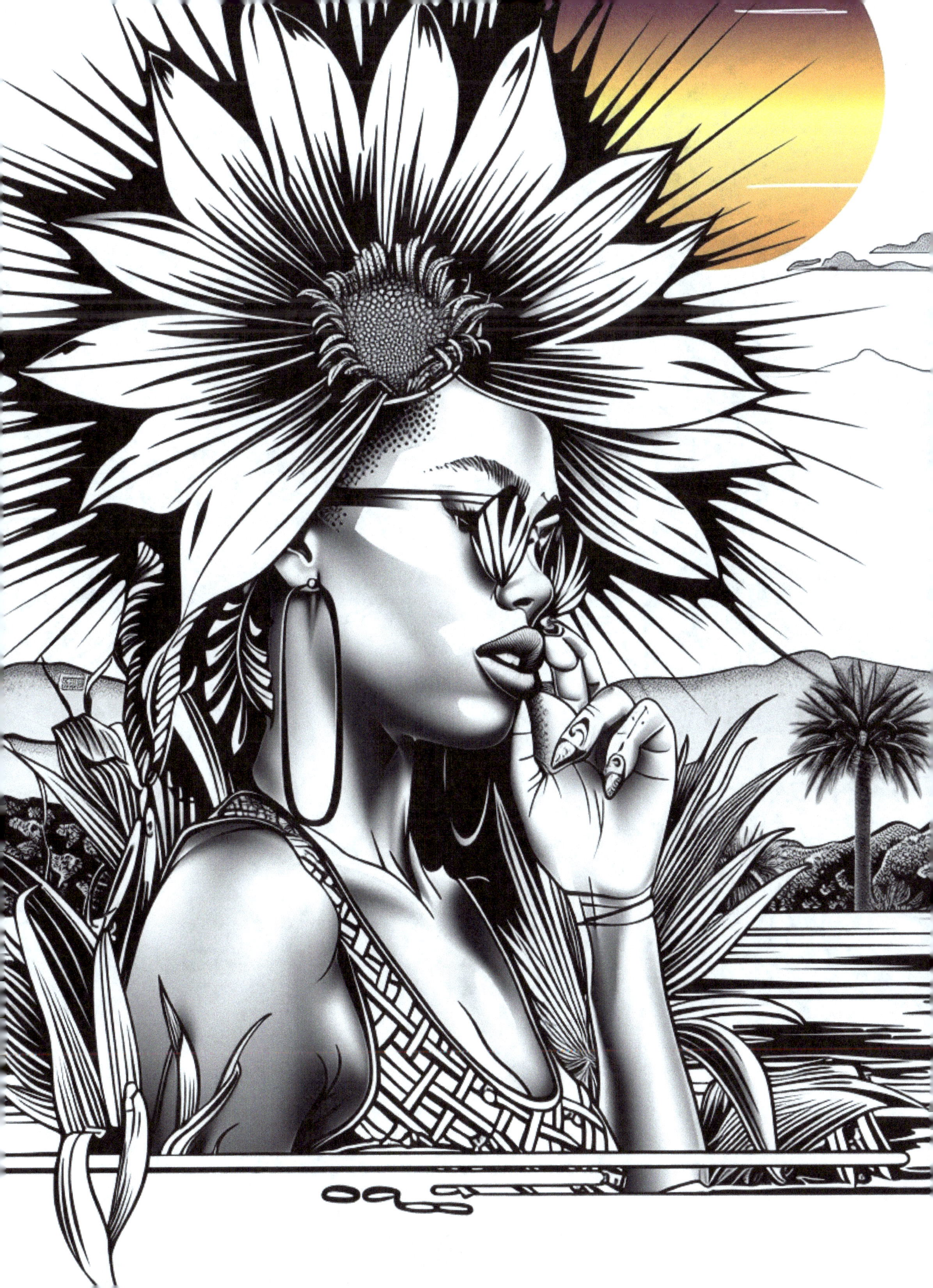

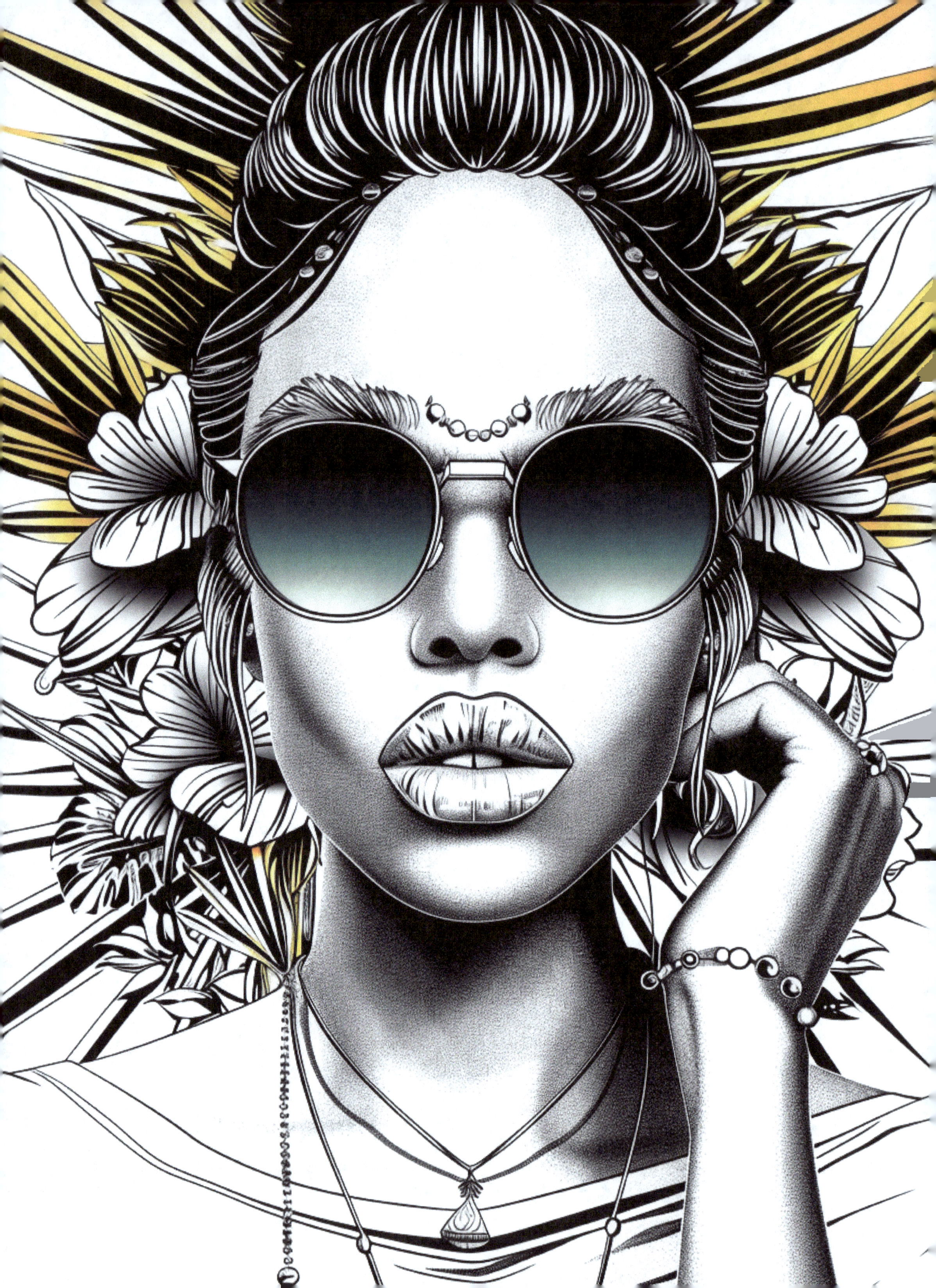

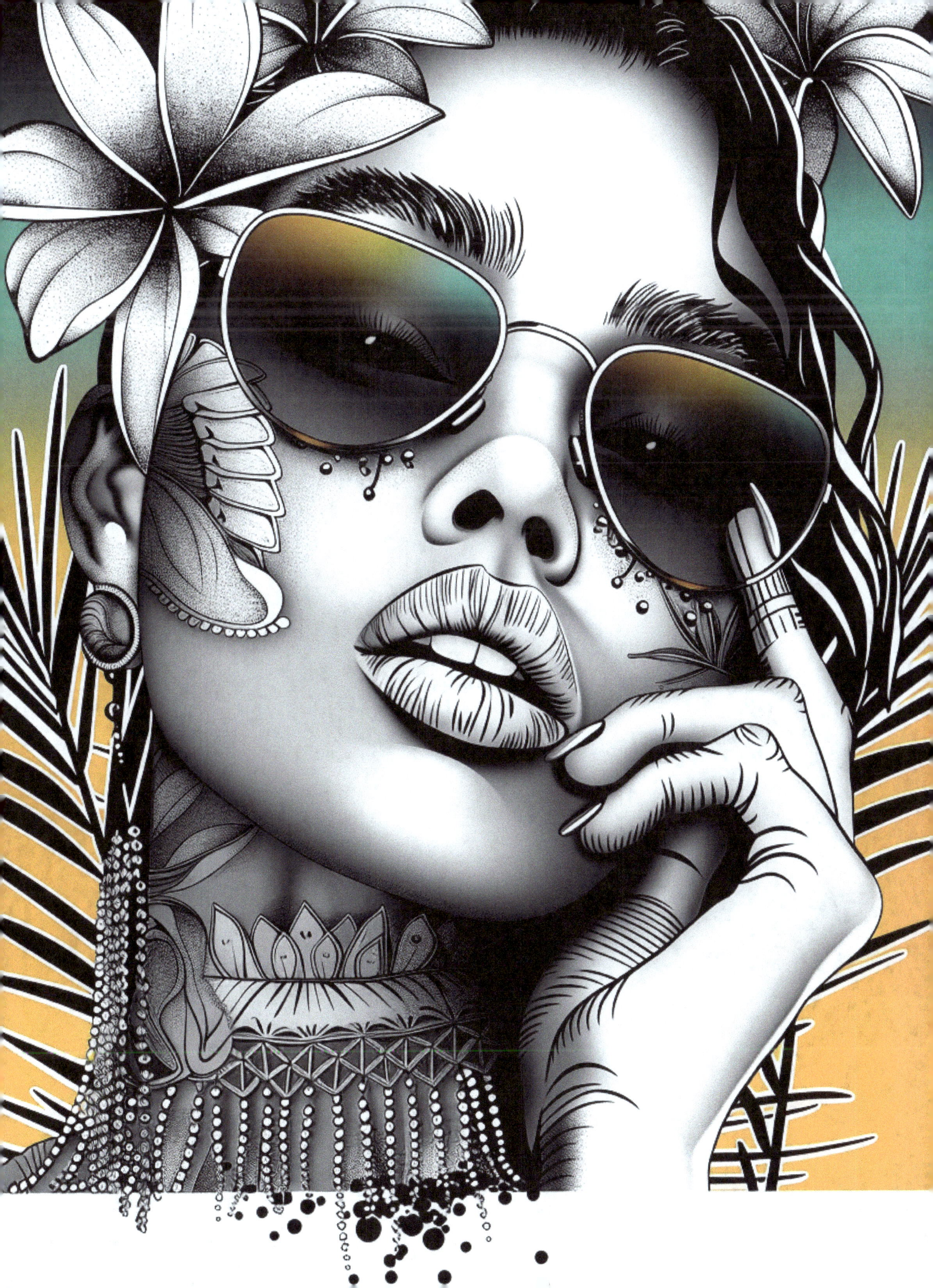

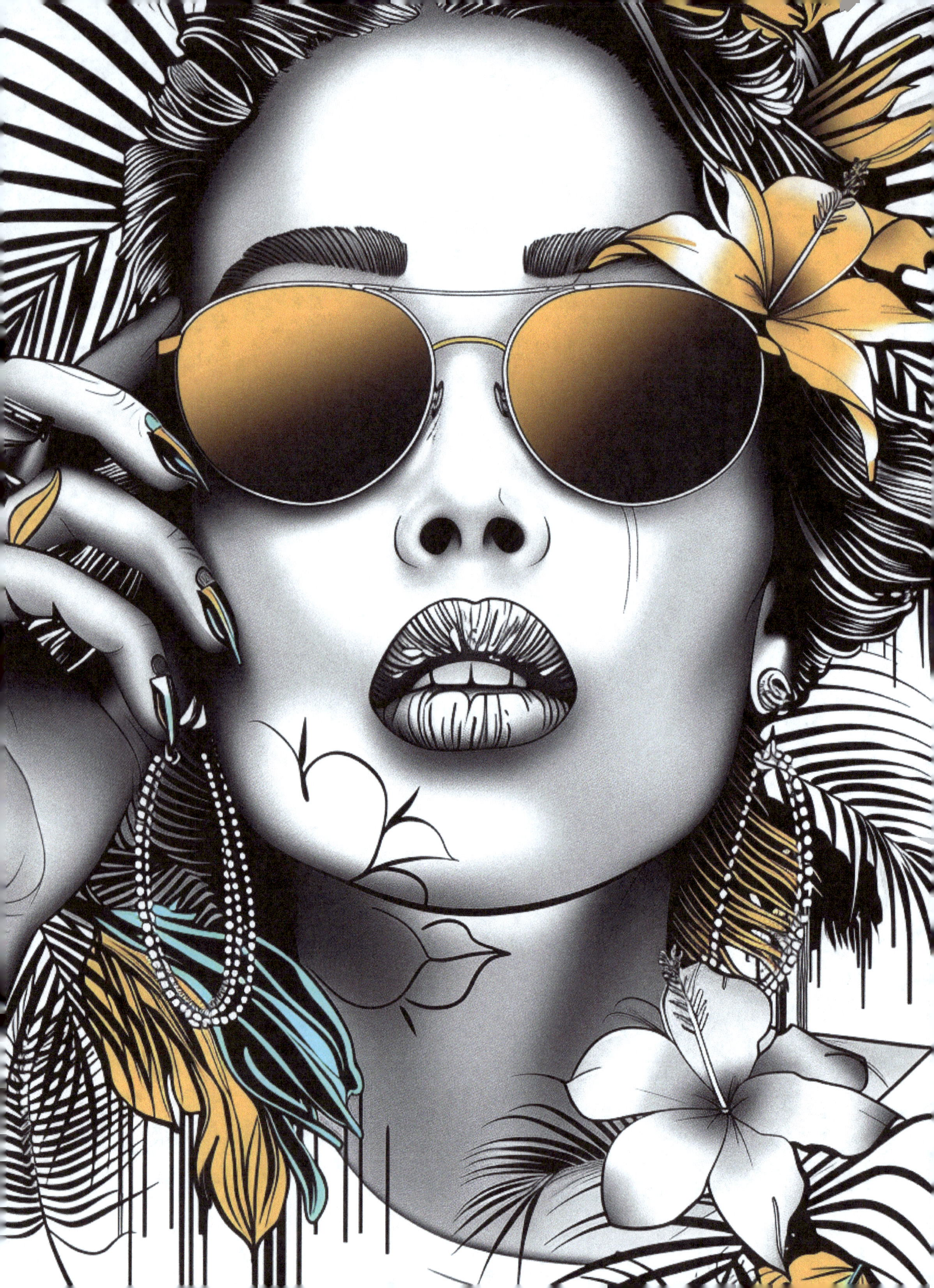

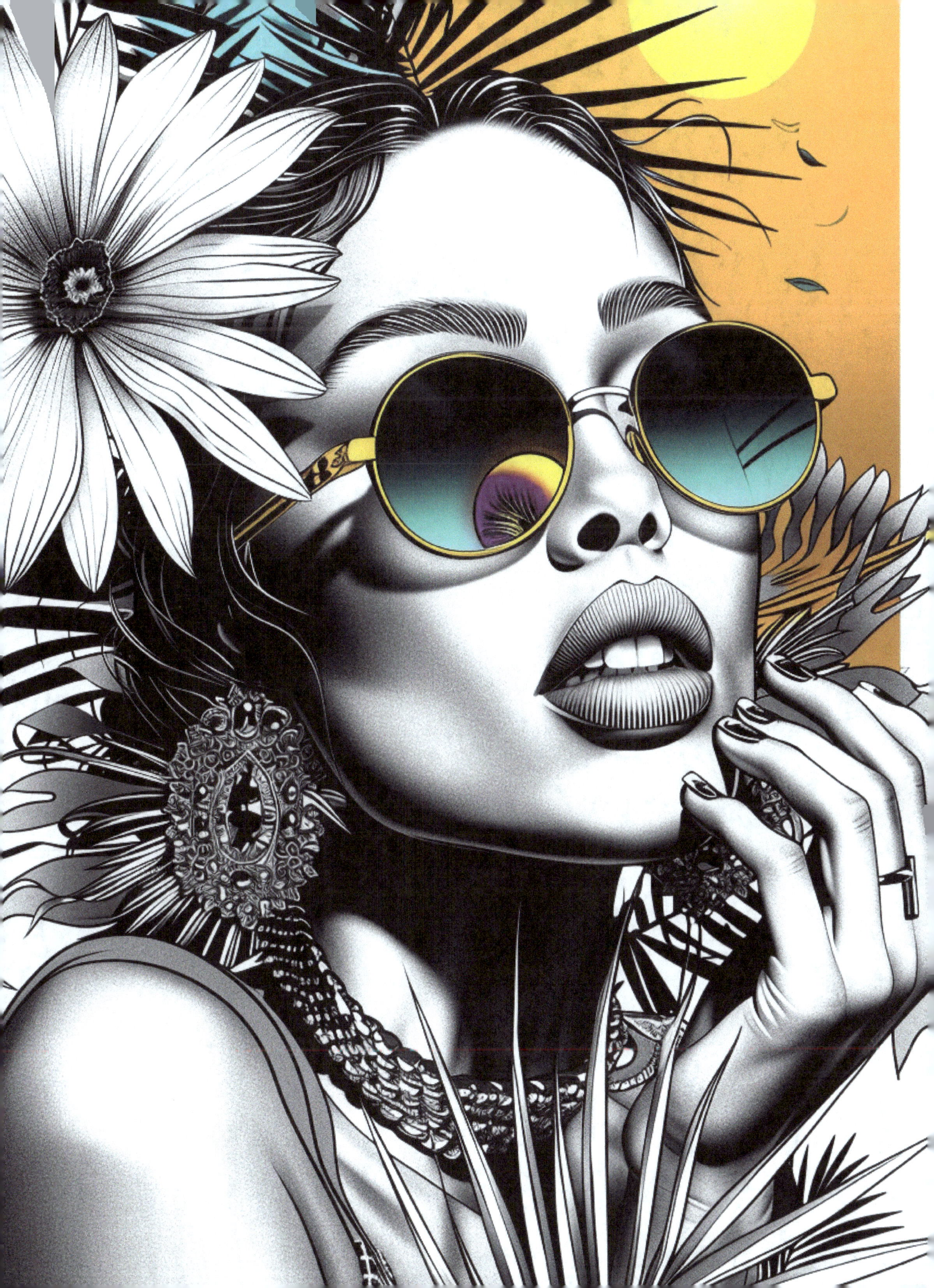

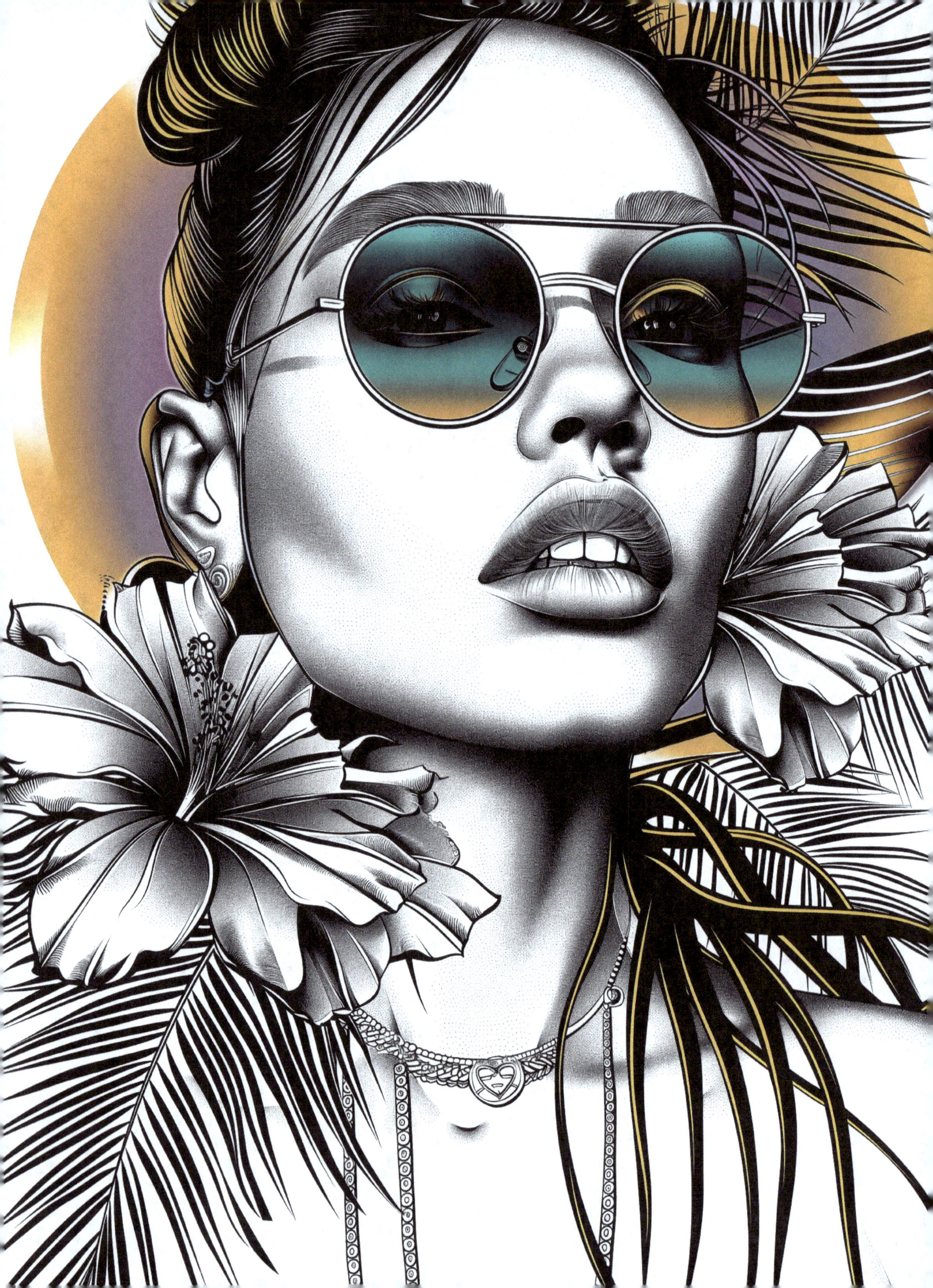

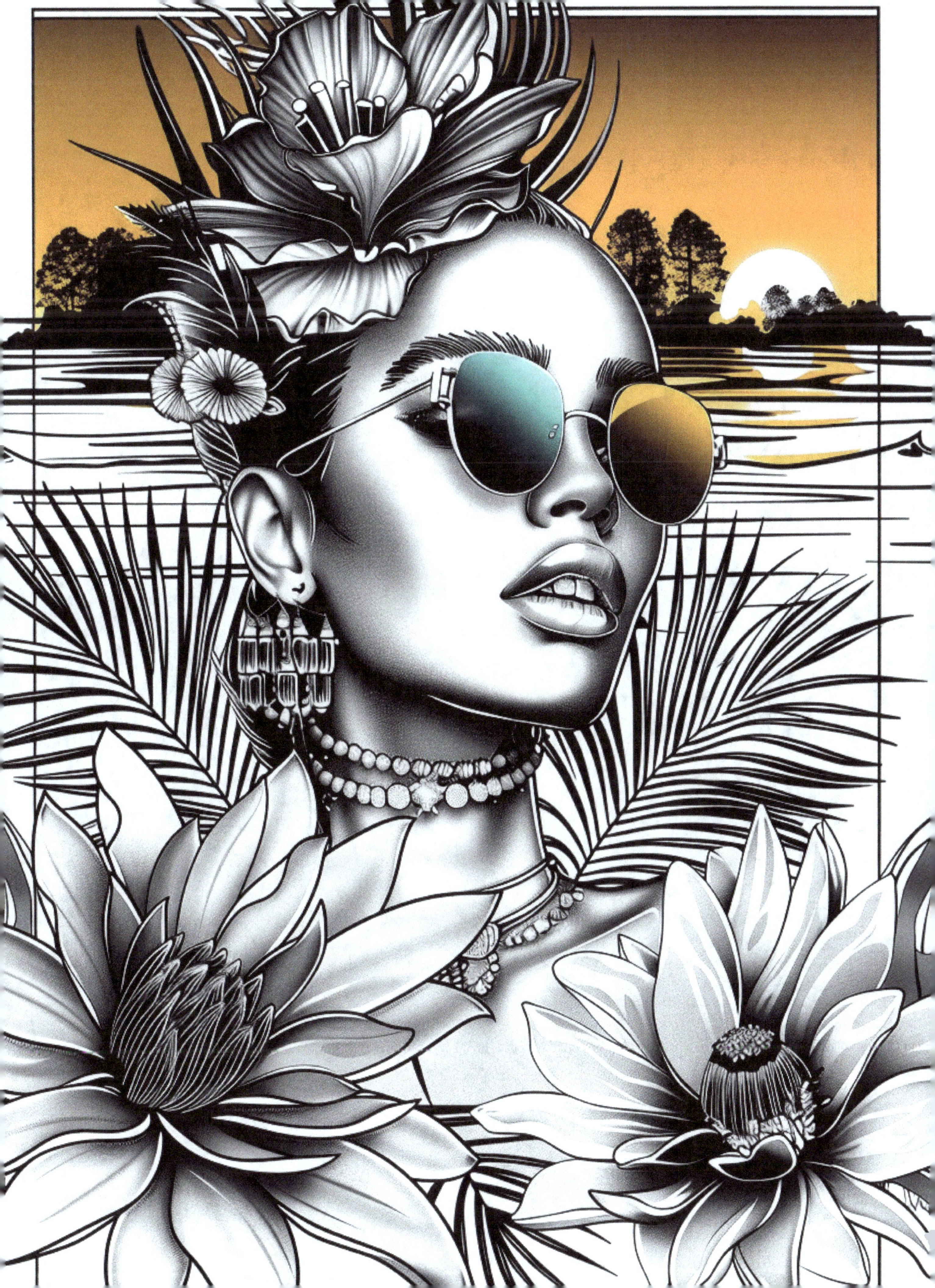

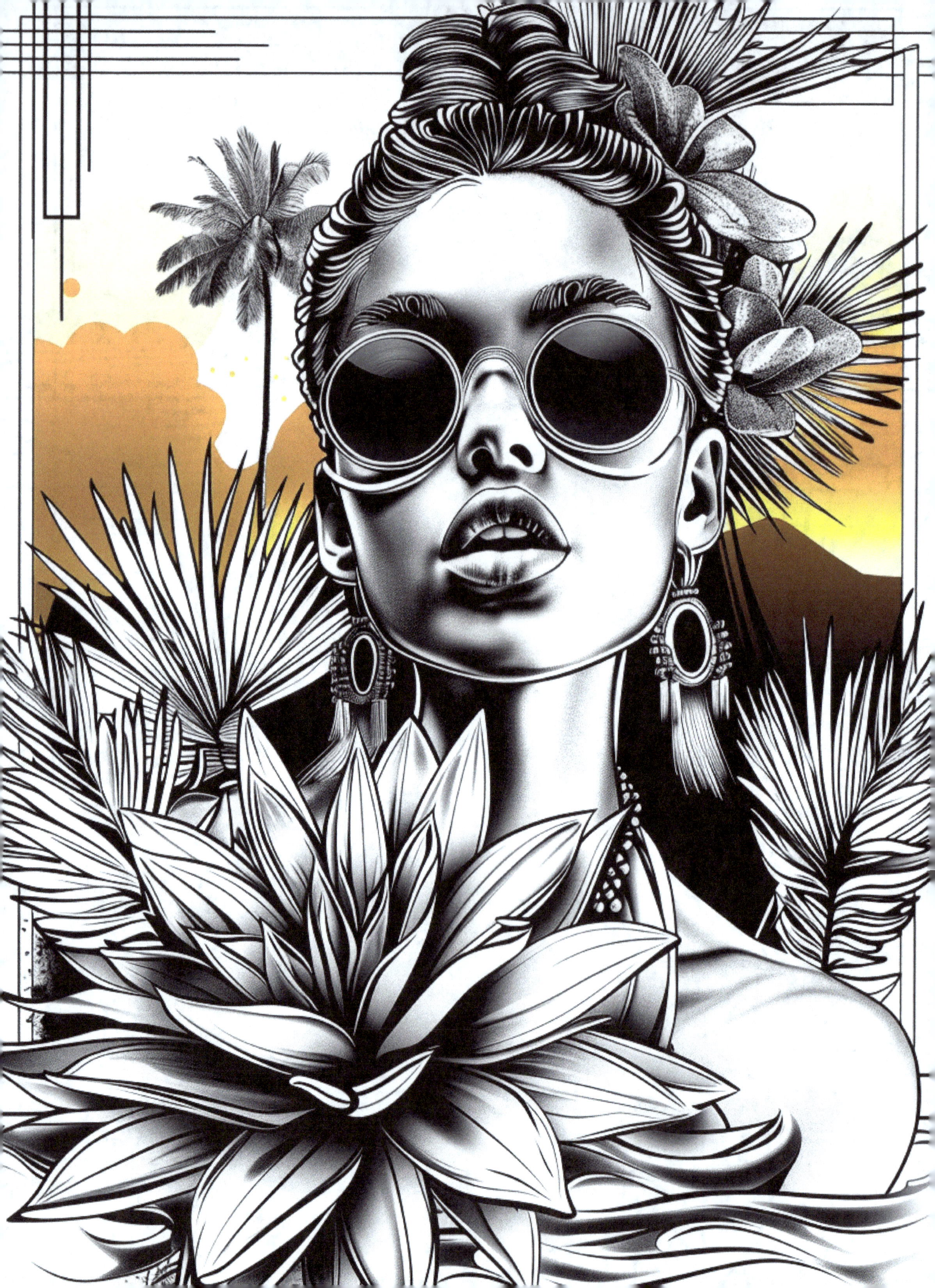

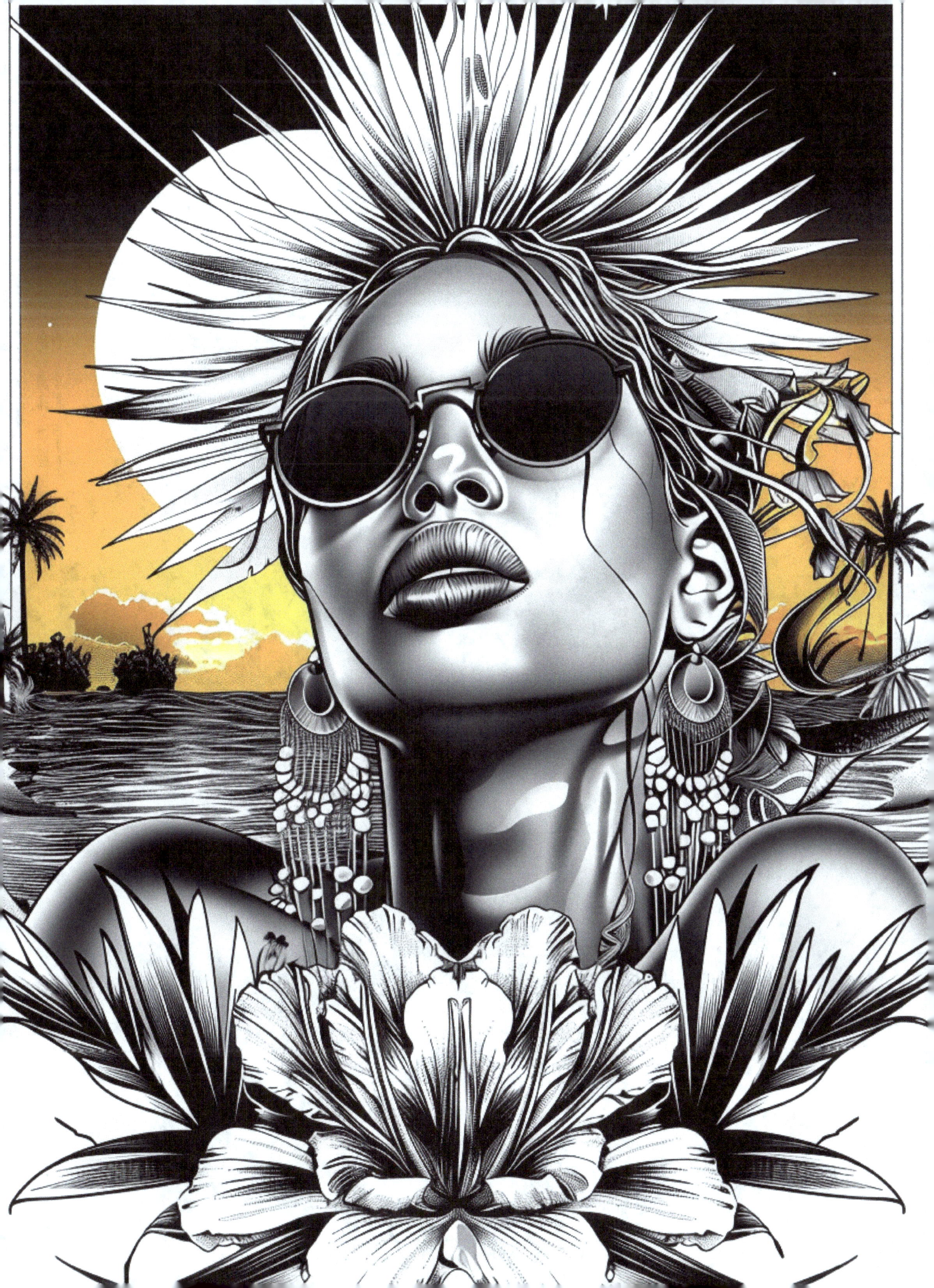

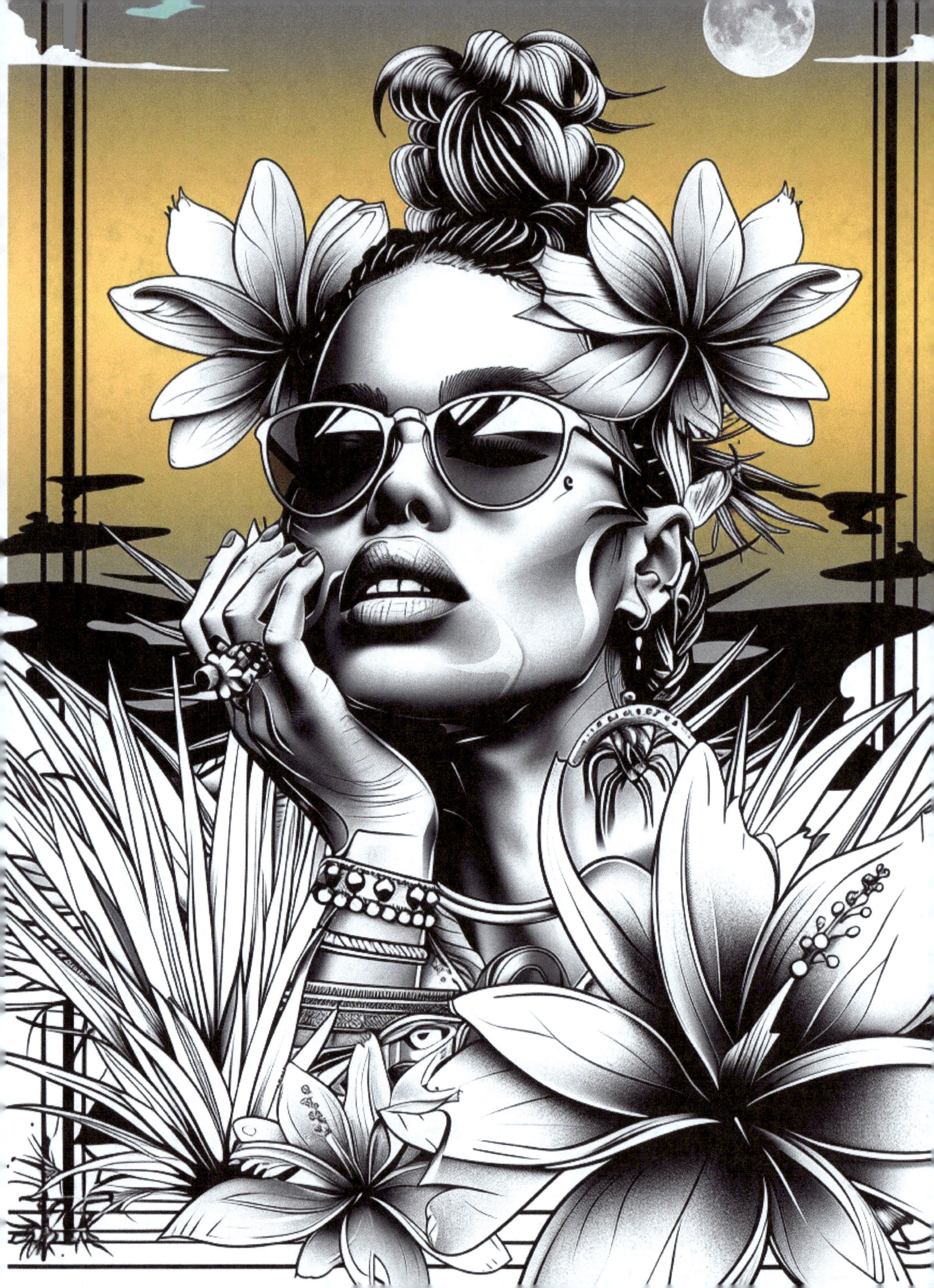

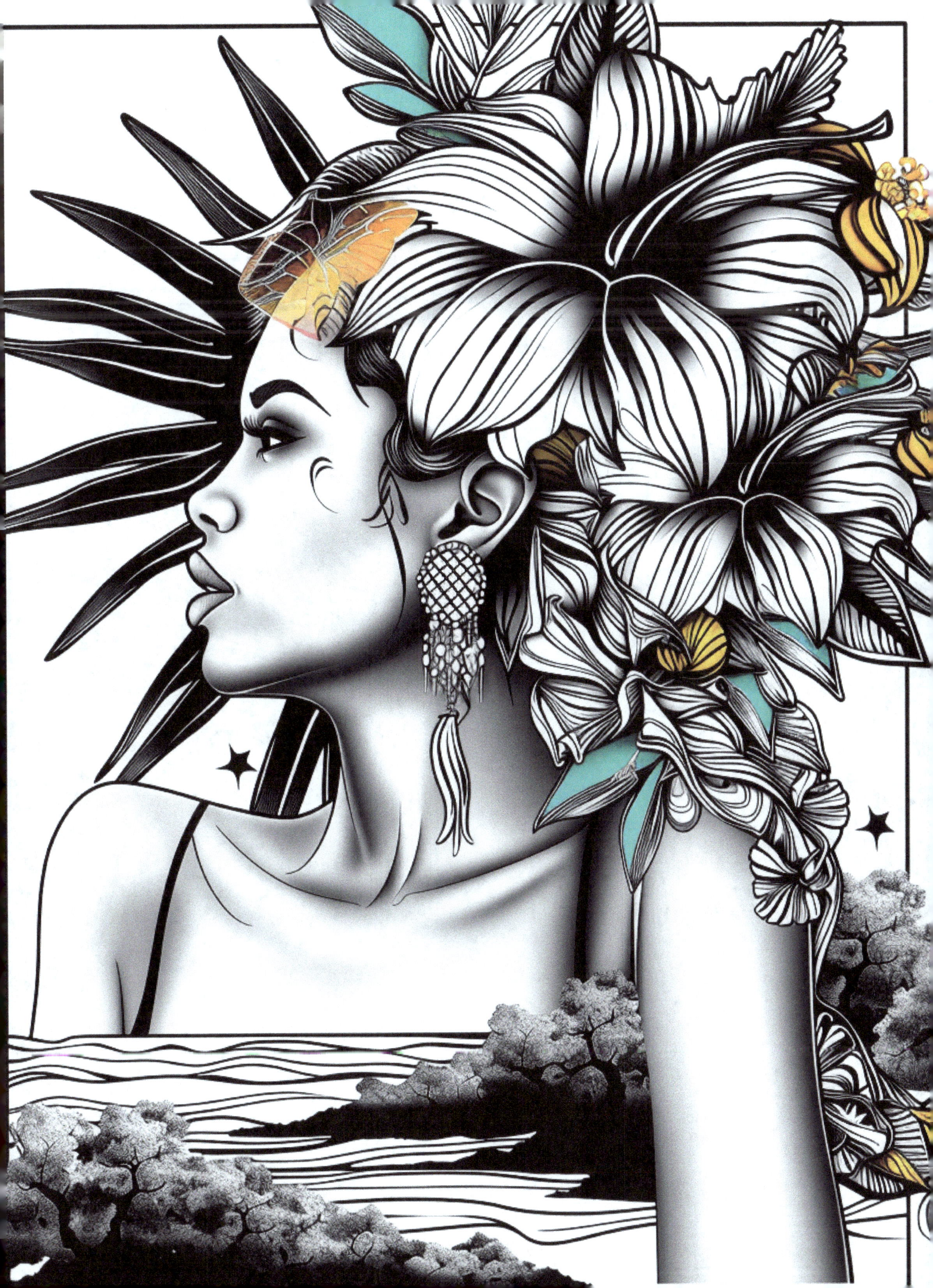

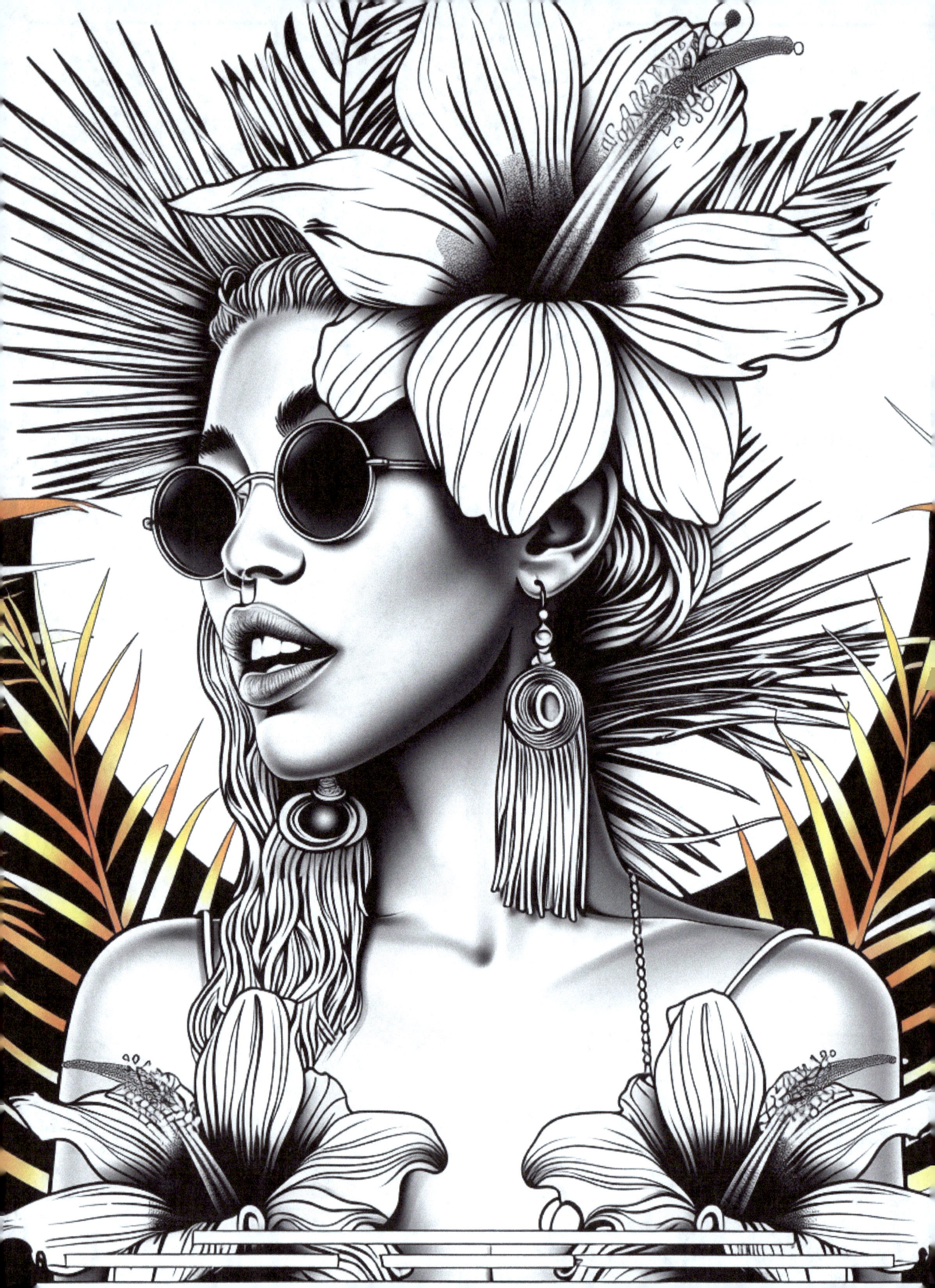

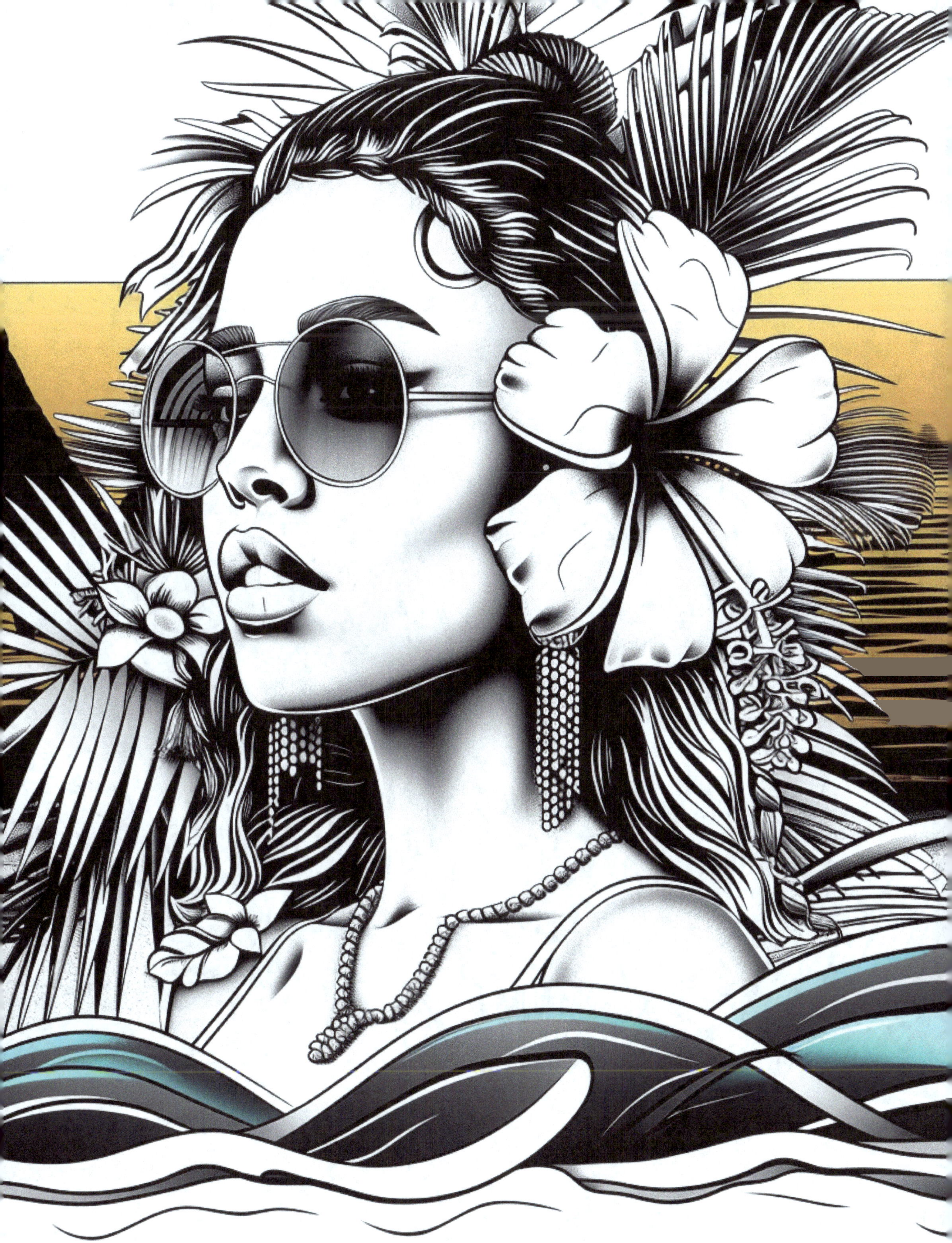

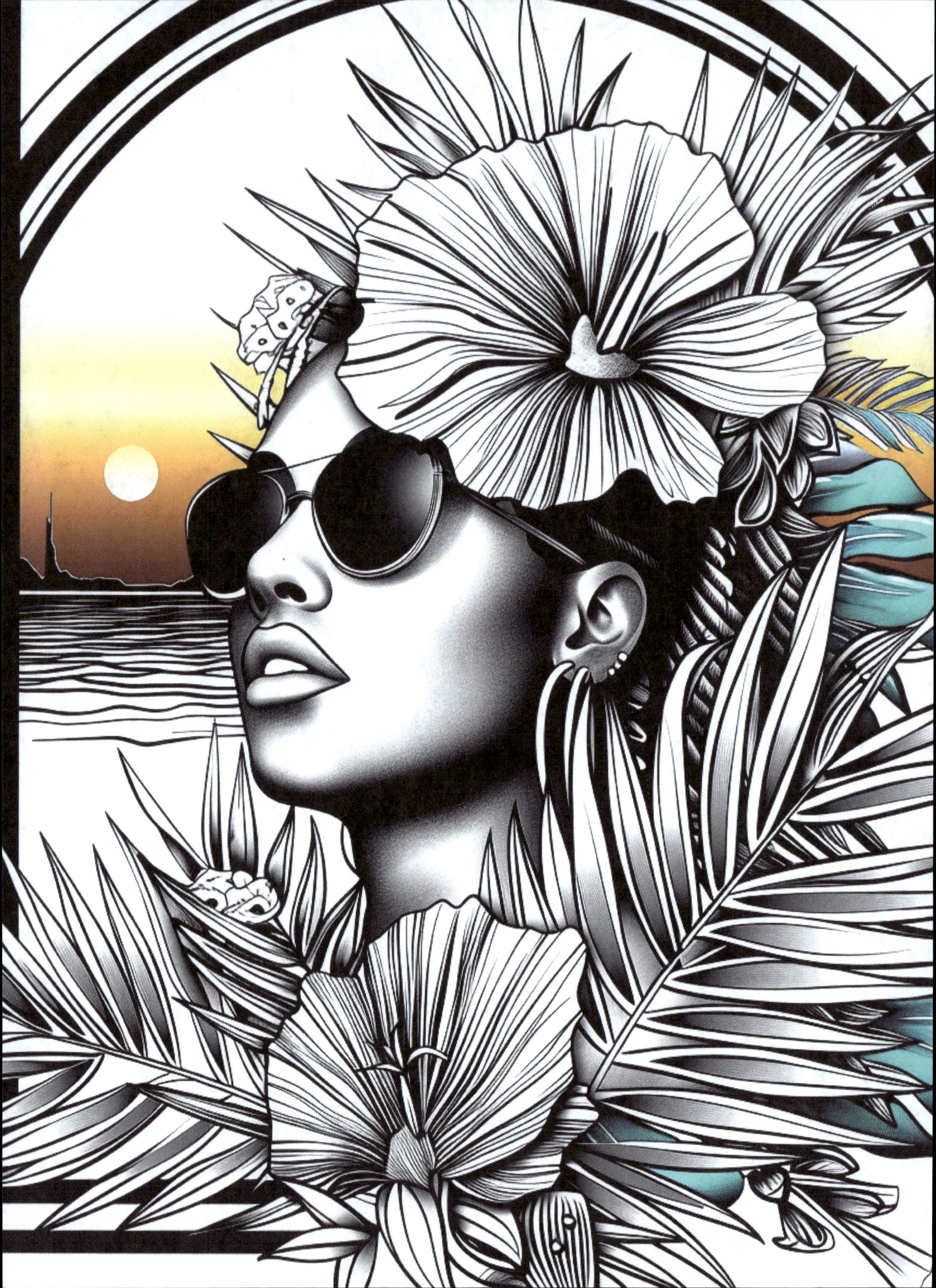

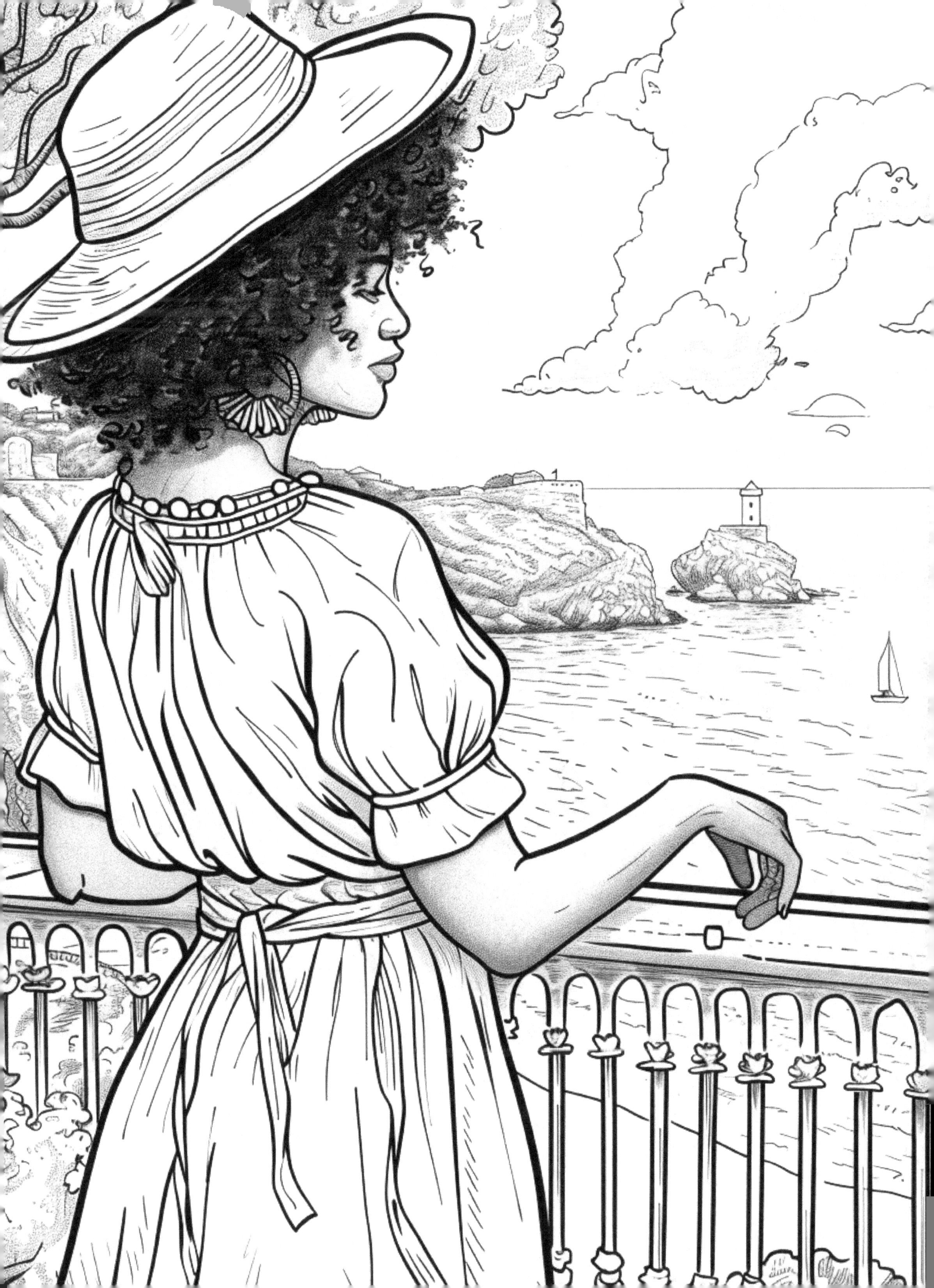

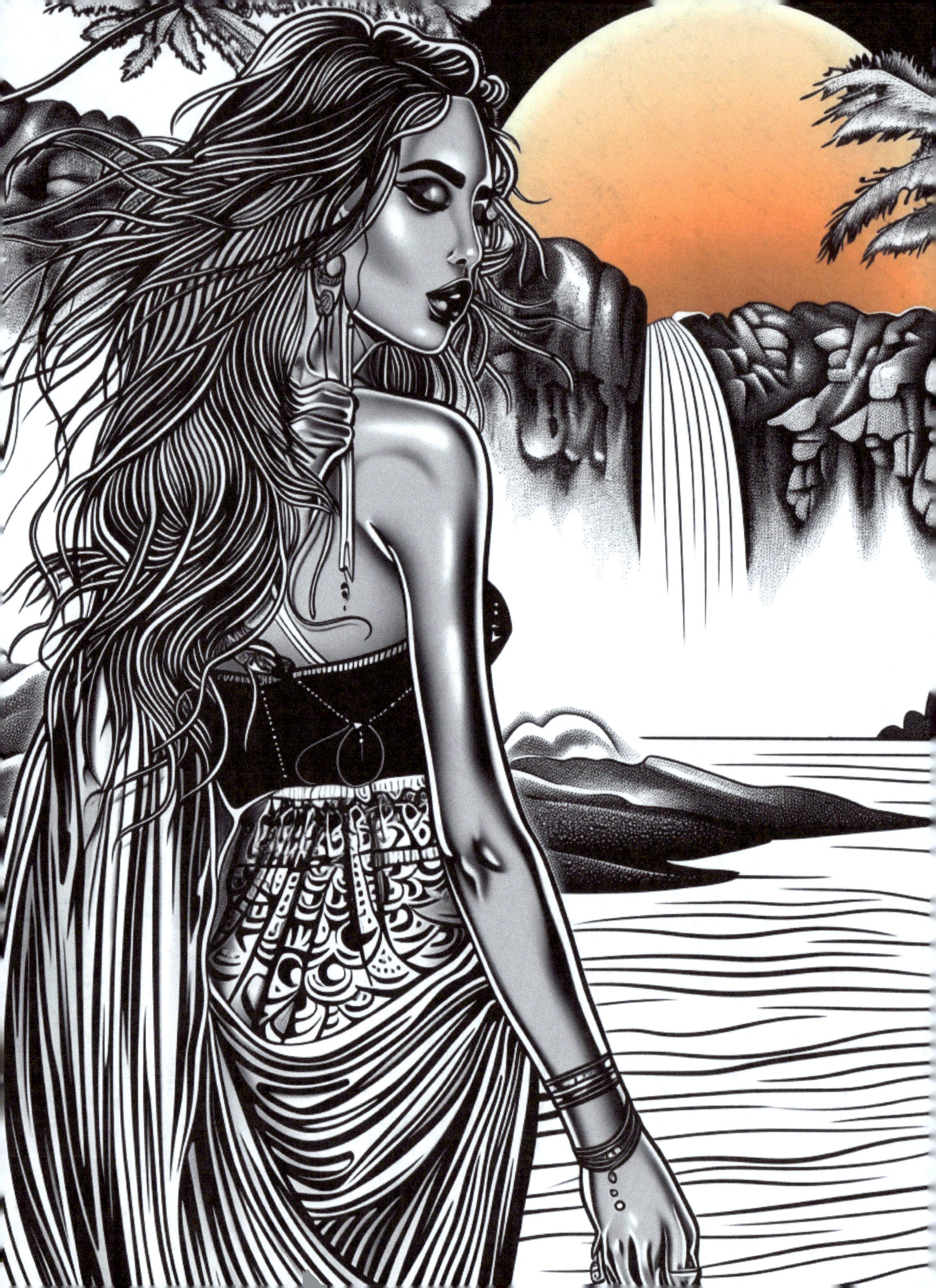

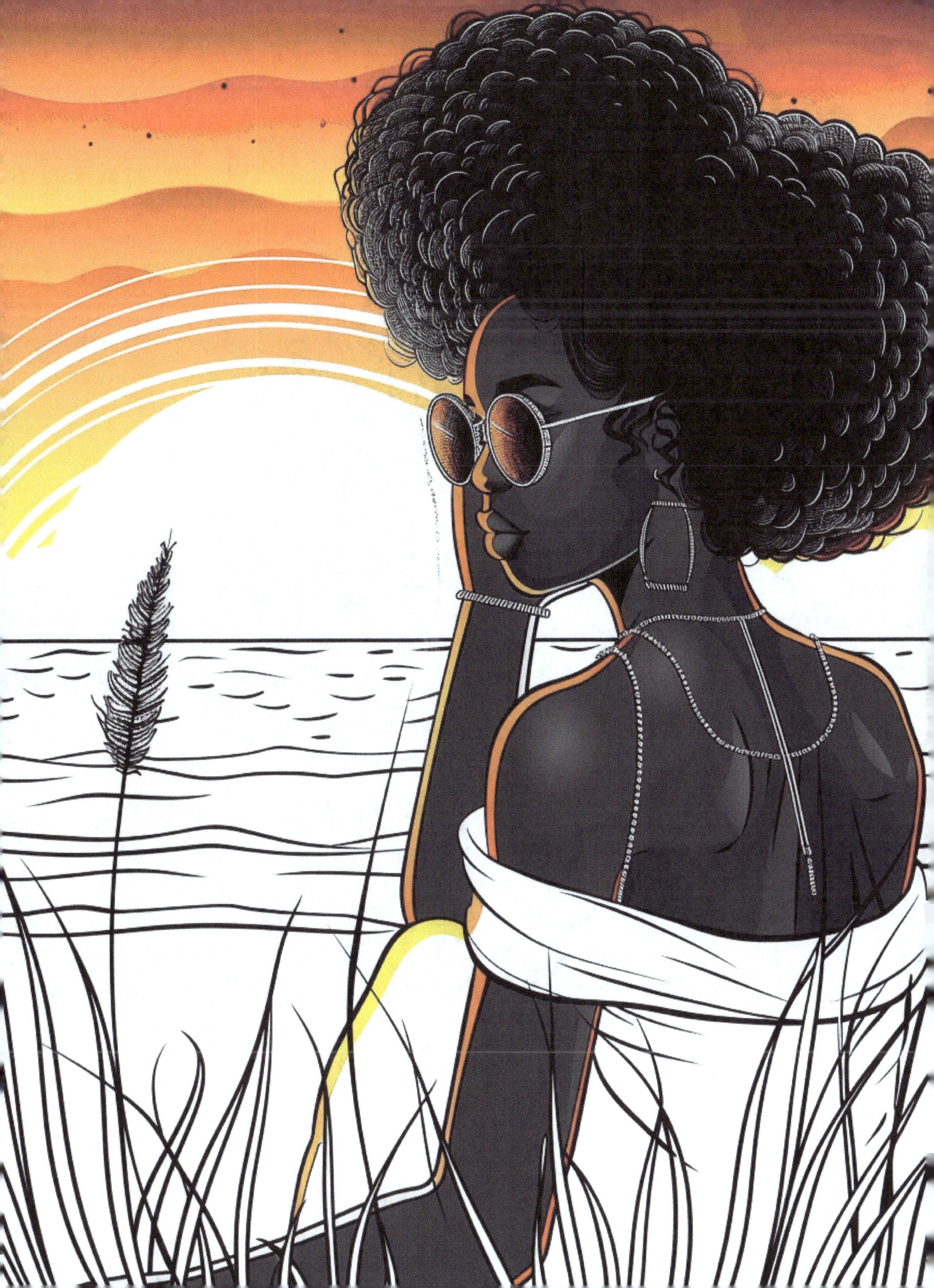

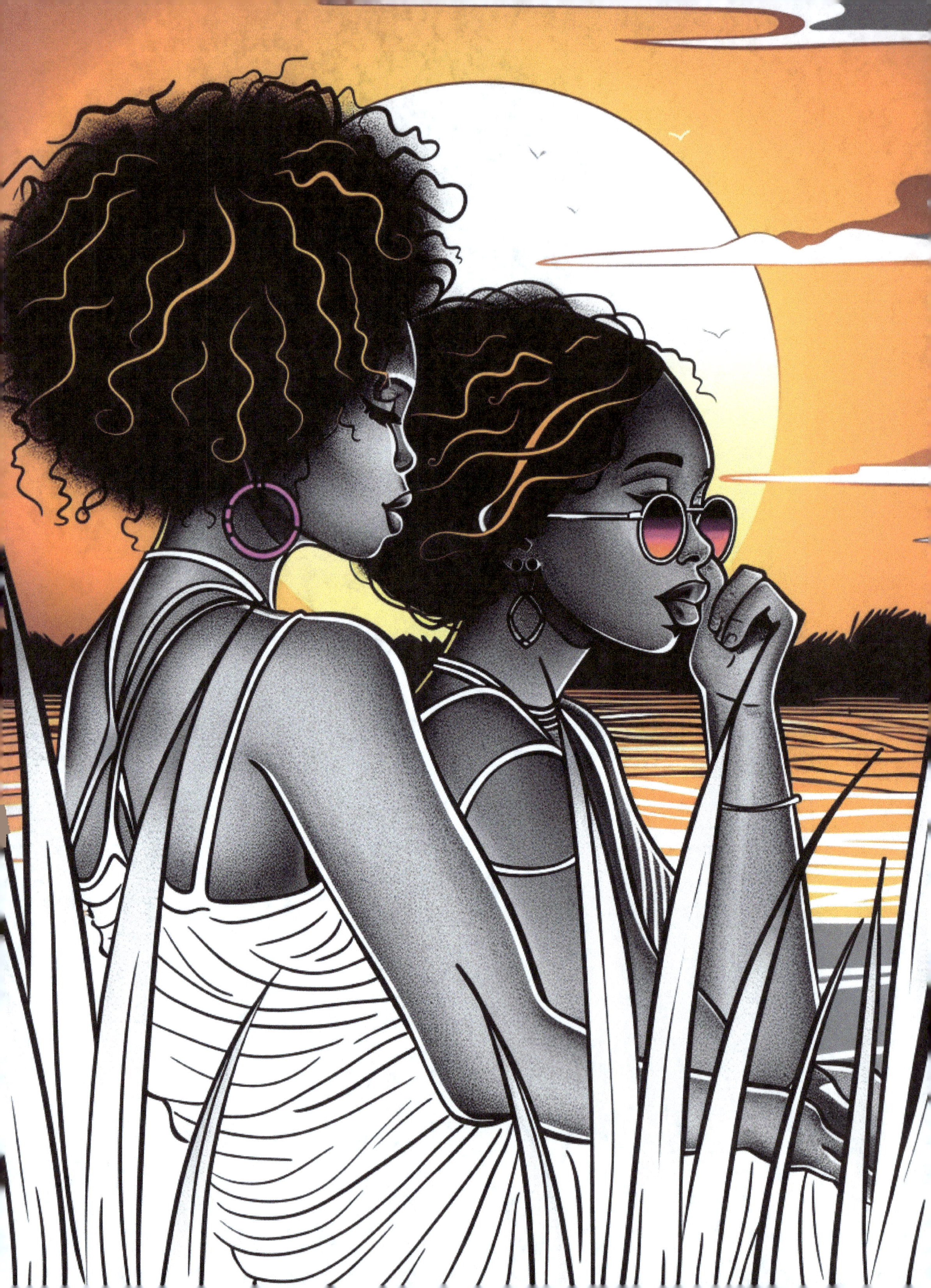

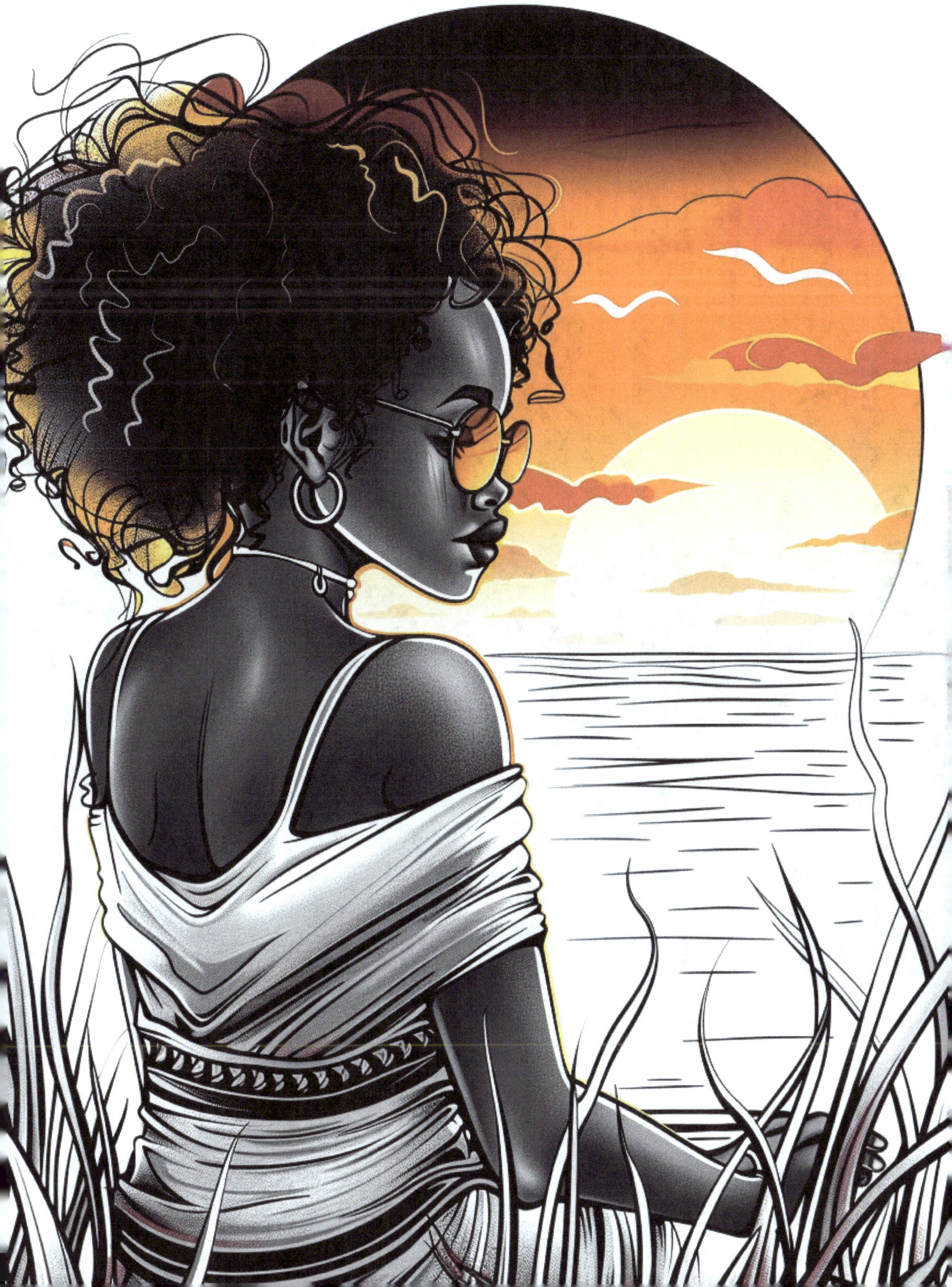

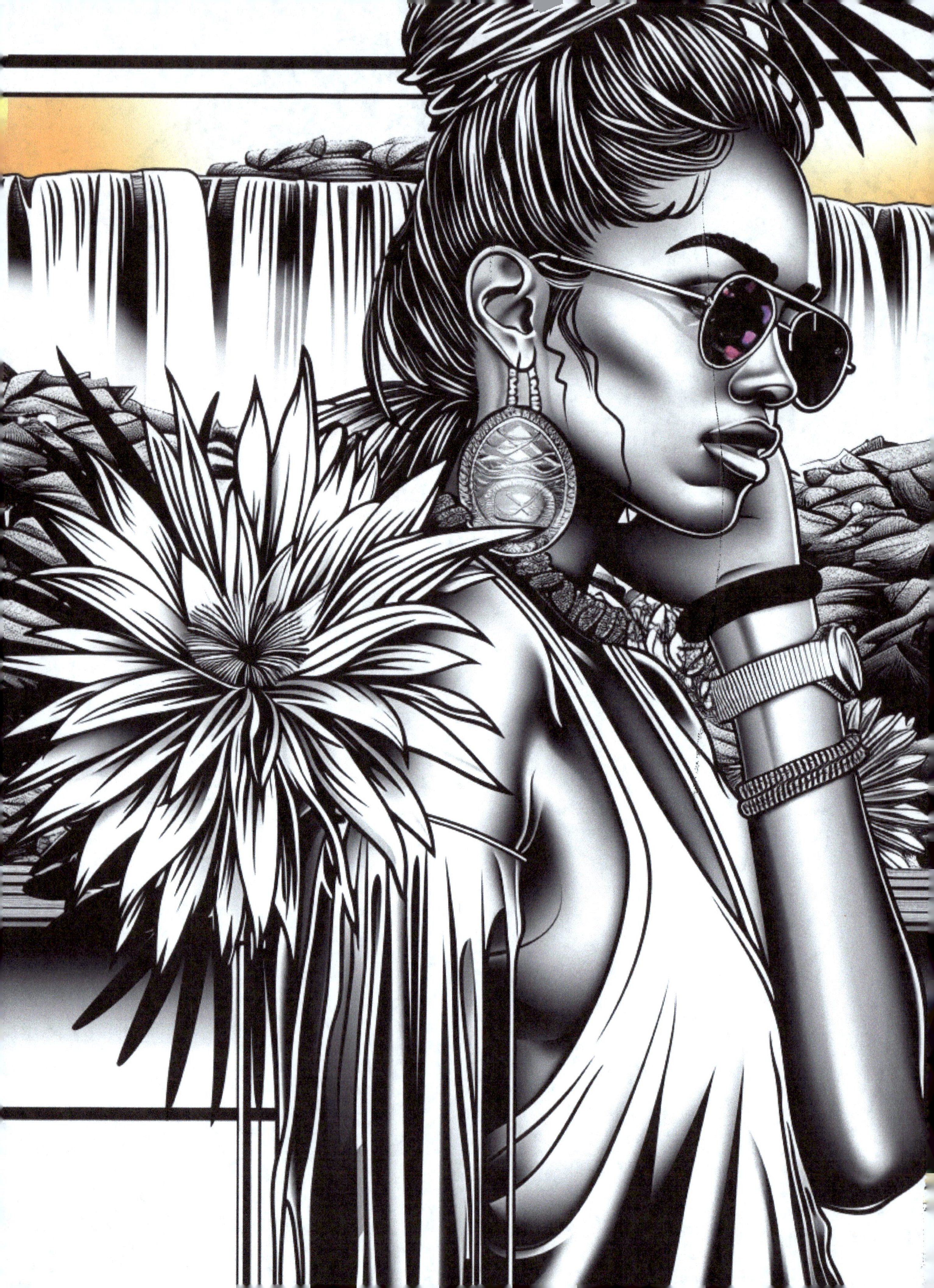

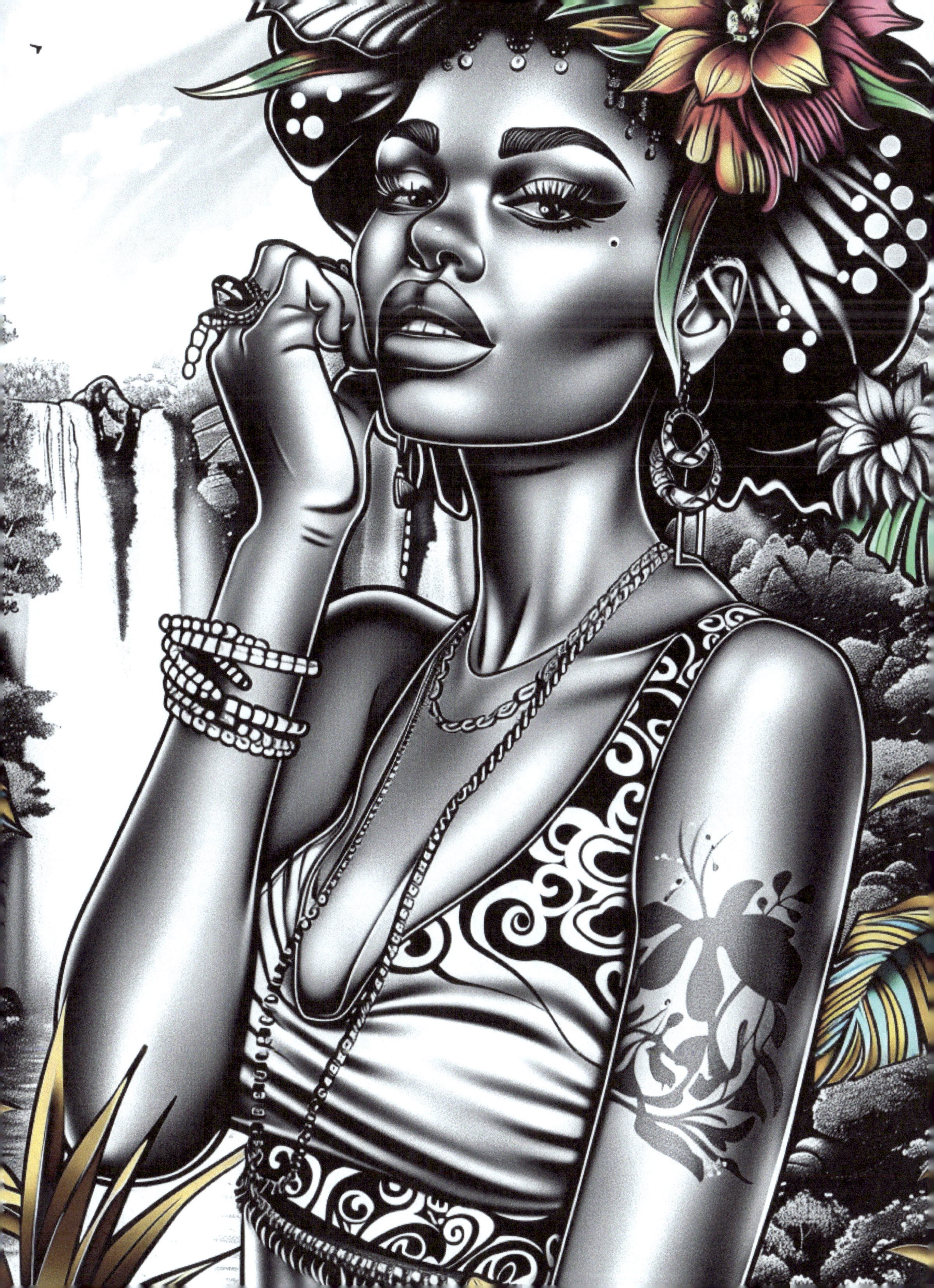

www.ingramcontent.com/pod-product-compliance
Lightning Source LLC
Chambersburg PA
CBHW060002230526
45472CB00008B/1912
9798327877733